Color Photography:
The Landscape

Color Photography: The Landscape

Hugo Schöttle

Amphoto
American Photographic Book Publishing Co., Inc.
Garden City, New York, 11530

This work was originally titled
Farbfotografie für jedermann: Die Landschaft
and published in Frankfurt, Germany.

Library of Congress Cataloging in Publication Data

Schöttle, Hugo.
Color Photography: The Landscape.

Translation of Farbfotografie für jedermann, die Landschaft.
Includes index.
1. Photography—Landscapes. 2. Color photography.
I. Title.
TR660.S3413 778.9'36 79-562

ISBN: 0-8174-2463-6

Manufactured in the United States of America

List of Photographers

Auer, Rudolf, **Germany, 26**
Baden, Susanne, **Denmark, 13**
Beheler, Noble B., **USA, 44**
Behnke, Julius, **Germany, 5, 52**
Berg, Kees van den, **Holland, 12, 15**
Champollion, Marc, **France, 14**
Chirol, Serge, **France, 49**
Cox, Donald S., **USA, 9**
Dünzl, Heribert, **Germany, 2, 4, 6, 11, 23, 30, 31, 36, 37, 38, 39**
Hartig, Siegfried, **Germany, 43**
Haug, Hans H., **USA, 46**
Hermann, Helmut, **Germany, 8**
Höpker, Thomas, **Germany, 10, 16**
Huber, Hans, **Germany, 34**
Katrecha, Dr. P. V., **India, 20**
Kaufmann, Josef, **Germany, 42**
Kühn, Bert, **Germany, 17**
Martin, André, **France, 21, 22**
Motal, Julius, **USA, 41**
Neumann, H. Jürgen, **Germany, 18**
Noordhoek, Wim, **Holland, 25**
Ollmann, Edgar, **Austria, 1**
Osterloh, Günter, **Germany, 47, 48**
Pauls, Uvo, **Germany, 3**
Piper, Jörg, **Germany, 51**
Reist, Dölf, **Switzerland, 32**
Roth, Hermann, **Germany, 40**
Sauser, Pierre, **France, 45**
Schiffmann, Hans, **Germany, 27**
Schöttle, Hugo, **Germany, cover, 33, 35, 50**
Stöcker, Hermann, Jr., **Germany, 24**
Weyer, Helfried, **Germany, 19, 28**
Wulff, Henning, **Canada, 7**
Zimmermann, M., **Holland, 29**

Table of Contents

Preface

Why should a photographer's experience of a landscape differ from the painter's or even the poet's, whose perceptions are artistically translated into verse? The question is certainly a valid one. Claude Monet painted his famous "Poplars on the Epte" in 1891. This work differs only slightly from the landscape photographed by André Martin (Photo 22). It is futile to philosophize about which of the two is "really" a work of art.

Landscape offers the amateur photographer a wide range of possibilities for exploring a chosen hobby and accommodating his or her interests and capabilities. There are no set rules on which way to approach the beauty and wonder of nature; and it can be a source of great satisfaction to capture sensual experiences in a color snapshot. The photographer who experiments with landscapes will soon realize that the difference between a direct experience of nature and its reflection in a color photo depends on photographic talents—on the photographer's ability to transform his or her perceptions into the concrete and visible form of a photo.

Nature should be appreciated in a very personal, subjective manner. This is not as difficult as it may sound, but it does require a conscious response to the subject and the patience to process this visual experience emotionally before pressing the shutter. Thus, only a true friend of nature can be a good landscape photographer. Nature offers plenty of opportunities for the self-realization of differing temperaments through photography—whether one is a cool aesthete, a dreamy romantic, a sensitive lyricist, or a passionate dramatist. Ideally the photographer's temperament, rather than the camera itself, should be the decisive factor in determining the quality of the photograph and in setting the style.

Landscape photography is not just a hobby for bright, sunlit days. No matter what the weather conditions may be, there are views of nature worth capturing. In a way, the change of seasons—the sprouting, maturing, and fading of vegetation—reflects the cyclical pattern of human existence. Sun, clouds, haze, fog, rain, and snow set the mood and lend a distinctive character to the landscape.

For the amateur photographer who wants to improve his or her style, nature offers a wealth of possible subjects and photographic "finger exercises." Taking good photos is like playing the piano. The finger exercises are followed by etudes of increasing difficulty, up to the "Gradus ad parnassum." True mastery is only a short step away. The examples in this book come from the journal *Leica Fotografie*. Rather than being a long-winded, detailed manual of instruction for beginners, this book is intended as a conversational introduction that hopes to inspire and provide a stimulus for photographic experimentation by offering the reader a wealth of possible subjects from which to choose. Perhaps once you start experimenting, you will not be able to stop.

Würzbach — Hugo Schöttle

1
Becoming a Landscape Photographer

COLOR VS. BLACK-AND-WHITE

An interest in landscape photography may be the result of any one of a variety of experiences. For one person it is the sudden overwhelming sensation of the beauty of nature; for another, an accidental glance in the viewfinder of a friend's camera or a spectacular photo seen hanging on the wall of a friend's home. Since you have acquired this book, your interest must have already been awakened. Perhaps you are somewhat dissatisfied with the pictures you have taken until now and are looking for some advice on how to take "better" pictures. This book hopes to offer some suggestions as to how this can occur.

Since 80 percent of all camera owners use color film, perhaps you have never taken black-and-white pictures. Rather than being at a disadvantage, you may find yourself a step ahead. Though still enthusiastically practiced in many photo clubs, black-and-white photography is becoming more and more a special, elite technique reserved for professionals and experts. Yet new technological developments in this field will be minimal. The future belongs to color. Perhaps you are an experienced amateur, with years of successful black-and-white photography behind you, who hopes this book will offer some helpful hints for your new adventure with color. You will soon realize the necessity of blocking out your experience with black-and-white, particularly in terms of your perception of form. Color photography will be a completely new medium for you. As consolation, perhaps it should be mentioned that color photography offers a wealth of possibilities for expressing yourself whatever you want to convey.

In black-and-white photography, the various gray tones produce a graphic-like quality that establishes the relationship between the forms. In color photography, composition is determined by the colors themselves to a large extent—if not exclusively so. Rather than a subtle contrast between light and dark shades of gray, an unending variety of hues and tones combine to give the picture its aesthetic and expressive character. Even a monochrome photo has expressive force that speaks to our sense of natural beauty (for example, Photos 12–20). It should be emphasized that monochrome landscape pictures—tone-in-tone compositions—are among the loveliest in color photography. Try for yourself. Choose any color you like—red, yellow, green, or blue. Some of the best examples of this technique are those of the famous American color photographer Peter Turner, whose preference for monochrome led him to use color filters. Many people are against such manipulation, but it seems a bit narrow-minded to view artificial color as a sin against the purity of natural representation. What *is* artificial? How a photo speaks to the viewer and the photographer is what is basically important. There is no right or wrong.

Is talent necessary? To create in color, you must not only think in colors but also experience them. A discussion of the symbolic significance of colors and their power to invoke certain emotions would be out of place here. Much has been written on this subject, and *Lüscher's Psychology of Color* (published by Lüscher-Test Testverlag, Basel, Switzerland) is recommended for the interested reader. Trusting one's own subjective perception of beauty is as important as knowing the precepts of a particular theory. An awareness of the temperature range of the color wheel is also important. That is, knowing that red through yellow to yellow-green includes the warm colors, and blue-green through blue to violet, the cool ones. These relationships between colors will often be referred to in describing and analyzing the various photographs included here.

DO YOU PERCEIVE COLOR CONSCIOUSLY?

This question is so simple that everyone automatically responds in the affirmative. Yet if your hobby is landscape photography, you should give your answer more careful consideration; the question is really not easy to answer. Certainly you know that a leaf is green, a flower is red, or yellow, and a tree trunk is brown, but what do you see when you go into the countryside over the weekend. You experience the forest and meadows and see the clear blue sky cut by the exhaust trail of an airplane flying overhead, but do you become aware of the different tones: of the harmony of green, yellow, blue, white, and red; of the innumerable colors of a meadow in springtime? Often you would like to capture this visual beauty and take it home with you. But if someone were to ask you even a few hours later what colors you had seen, you would probably only be able to provide a vague description, particularly of those colors that are a mixture of several hues, as for example, "dandelion yellow."

The amateur landscape photographer must learn to see and think in color, to differentiate between the delicate nuances of color, and to look for subjects that are not only interesting, but that also offer balanced color compositions. Color is everywhere, but good color compositions are not easy to find. Perhaps the various examples included in this book will help you in your search by focusing your attention on the effect colors have on each other. The more delicate the colors and hues, the more natural their harmony within a landscape setting, and the more difficult it becomes to capture them in a photograph.

Generally speaking, it takes a blood-red sunset to awaken people from their normal lethargic and passive perception of color, to arouse the exclamation, "Isn't that lovely"! The sun, nature's greatest light meter, must pour a whole bucketful of color into the sky in order to stimulate a reaction that is consciously registered first by our eyes, then by our perception of color, and finally by our understanding and our emotions. It is no wonder then that sunsets are among the most photographed scenes, and that an entire chapter in this book has been devoted to this subject.

Sunsets are beautiful, but nature has numerous other, possibly even more beautiful, color compositions to offer—although "beautiful" is a relative concept. What is "beautiful"? What is "more beautiful"? These are questions that each person must answer individually. Certainly any comparison between two subjects as different as a glowing sunset and a delicate spring landscape is problematic. The evaluation of a color picture is based on criteria other than just the popularity of its subject matter or the intensity of the colors.

To see in color also means to differentiate. Green is not just simply green. Nature offers a complete spectrum of delicate nuances of a certain hue, and it is important to distinguish between light green, dark green, blue-green, yellow-green, and so on. When mixed with other colors, the result may be olive-green or turquoise. Changes in light during the course of the day have an important effect on color values. The morning and evening sun emphasize the warm colors, mixing some red with the green and transforming the blue into violet. Color opposites are important as well. Where the golden yellow cornfield is shaded by leafy trees, it acquires a gentle shimmer. The blue of the sky is reflected in the depth of a lake or from the rugged snow-capped peaks of a mountain range (Photo 32). The blue cast of a winter landscape is not caused by a defective film. The sky's reflection is real. Counteracting this blue with a red filter may help keep theoretical precepts intact (snow is white), but it modifies reality. In addition, the different color films are calibrated to varying color temperatures. Some daylight films favor reds—the warm tones—and others favor blues—the cool colors. It is important to remember that daylight films are calibrated to a medium color temperature (approximately 5400 degrees Kelvin [K]). Tungsten films are calibrated to the warmer color temperature of incandescent light (about 3200 K). Thus, many factors influence the color composition of a landscape.

COLOR PHOTOGRAPHY OR "COLORED" PHOTOGRAPHY?

The person who requests a "colored" film betrays an ignorance of color photography through his or her choice of words. For the experienced amateur photographer, a disparaging reference to "colored" pictures is harsh criticism indeed. Such a description implies that a photo has too many colors that clash too harshly with each other, thereby destroying the effect created by the subject matter. A colorful autumn leaf can be a masterpiece when set against a fairly monochrome background; but if seen amidst an assortment of intense autumn colors, the picture becomes too colorful and the singular beauty of the leaf itself is completely lost.

We have come a long way from the old-fashioned dictum that every color picture needs a "red spot." This so-called rule must have originated with a photographer who had only a vague notion of color composition. Or perhaps the thesis of the red spot was the slogan of a clever advertising manager who wanted to emphasize the particularly brilliant red color attainable with a certain brand of color film. In any case, this dictum was printed in many books and unfortunately influenced several generations of color photographers in the wrong way.

Harmony and Dissonance. Harmony and dissonance are important in color photography, just as they are in music. The pure intervals of music (fourth, fifth, octave) are like the primary colors—yellow, red, and blue. These colors cannot be obtained by mixing other colors but can themselves be mixed to produce the secondary colors—orange, violet, and green. (In photography these are referred to as yellow, magenta, and cyan.) All other colors can be produced from these primary and secondary colors, even the finest nuances that are barely detectable with the naked eye. Those interested in pursuing this subject further should consult Harald Mante's book *Farbdesign* (Color Design), published by Otto Maier Verlag, Ravensburg, Germany.

The advantages of monochrome color patterns; the appeal of tone-in-tone designs; the beauty of a pastel composition, such as an overcast but bright sky; a diffuse light situation; and haze or fog have already been mentioned. The danger of taking a "colorful" picture in such a situation is minimal. The danger is much greater with a clear blue sky and a blazing sun, especially when one follows the wise old saying, "Keep the sun at your back." The effect produced is rather like illuminating the landscape with a huge spotlight; the multiplicity of forms and colors becomes the picture's downfall, as it acquires the character of a colorful rag carpet. But this very same rag carpet becomes photogenic when photographed with the sun at one side or even when taken against the sun. *The sun at your side or facing you* is the motto to follow for good landscape photos. However, in this book, there are only a few examples of photos taken in full sunlight, which just goes to show that good landscape photography is not at all dependent on sunny weather.

The critical landscape photographer should strive for a composition with few colors and distinct forms, unless he or she is attempting to achieve a certain harmony with a multiplicity of flashy colors and the use of creative photographic techniques (Photos 24 and 26). It is easy to imagine how different these images would have been if the photographer had not added an artistic hazy touch to these photos. In experimental landscape photography, the line between kitsch and art, between colorfulness and color, is sometimes very narrow (Photos 47–52).

IN SEARCH OF SUBJECTS

Good landscape photos are no accident. Choosing interesting subjects, which are abundant, is only the first step. A creative approach is required, in addition to first-class equipment (camera, various lenses, good color film), and proper light conditions. The sun need not be shining, as has already been discussed. Many excellent photos have been taken in the rain. Some photographers choose their subject, frame it quickly in the viewfinder, click the shutter, and the landscape is captured on film. Others spend days wandering around a certain group of trees, snapping dozens of shots without ever being satisfied. The "happy medium" is somewhere between these two extremes of complete unpretentiousness and fanatical obsession.

Photography is a question of temperament, and it is not easy to make suggestions for locating subjects. A subject that comes as a revelation for one photographer may say nothing at all to another, or even seem unappealing. Everyone must do his or her own looking. Landscape artists of days gone by often carried a frame that served as a viewfinder and aided them in locating subjects. It is somewhat easier today, as a photographer need only focus the camera in order to see whether a certain picture is worthwhile. Sometimes small vest-pocket-size binoculars can aid in the search for subjects by bringing details into the field of vision, which would otherwise go unnoticed. However, they show a telescopic view of a scene, which more or less corresponds to the effect created by a 400 mm lens. A close-up view of the details may still be worthwhile, though, to help a photographer create exactly the picture that he or she wants.

Experience has shown that some of the most beautiful subjects are often seen only at "second glance." What does this mean? Perhaps you have taken what seemed to be a good shot, only to discover the flaws in the developed photo or slide. Maybe you should try the shot again. Landscape subjects can often haunt you for many years as "uncompleted works" that simply do not permit a definitive "once and for all" shot to be taken. Sooner or later one tires of a certain subject and moves on to the next, only to start the same process from the beginning again. The process of becoming a successful landscape photographer is a gradual one.

After learning to "see" in color, you will suddenly notice a change in the way you approach nature. On a walk through the woods, you will no longer find yourself thinking about unanswered correspondence or plans for the coming week. There is no time for such thoughts anymore. Your great adventure has begun. You begin to notice small details at the side of the path which escaped your eyes before. The details of a scene begin to occupy your thoughts and become a new experience. Your new pattern of thought will become apparent to you when people ask repeatedly what you are thinking. Your repeated pauses to consider the image in the viewfinder may annoy a friend, whose idea of an afternoon stroll may be somewhat different. This can be a critical moment. It may be that your enthusiasm for landscape photography will transform you into a "lonely walker." However, a clever move can counteract this trend. Give your friend a camera too; perhaps he or she will become as enthusiastic as you are.

SYMMETRY, ASYMMETRY, AND MIXED FORMS

There are people who are at peace with themselves and others who are not. This dictum applies equally to the language of the photo-geometric world of forms, for there are balanced subjects (symmetric) and others that are out of balance (asymmetric). Just as with people, one indicates peace and harmony, and the other, tension and dissonance. Mixed forms with elements of both symmetry and asymmetry also exist. Such mixtures are the general rule in landscape photography. It is also necessary to distinguish between symmetry of form on the one hand and of color on the other. Symmetry of form can be counterbalanced by asymmetrical colors, and vice versa.

First, it is necessary to consider form, limiting yourself to the format of a photo; that is, either a rectangle or a square. For the most part, the square can be excluded, since this form occurs only rarely in landscape photography. There is not a single square picture in this book, and only one even approaches a square (Photo 36).

The Format. The reason for this is simply that the viewfinder of a camera always corresponds to the 24 × 36 mm format of the film, and the photographer generally tries to compose a picture so that it is as "format-filling" as possible. Altering the natural proportions of the picture by cutting the film is done only in rare cases. In spite of this unwillingness to deviate from the standard format, it is a good idea to break away from this force of habit occasionally. Many subjects gain additional tension and expressive force when seen in an extremely narrow and upright frame. So try setting a river landscape in a very wide horizontal frame, for example; or set a slender young birch tree in a narrow, upright frame and watch its slender proportions gain an upward force.

Symmetry creates the feeling of peace, harmony, and balance. Generally speaking, this feeling can be achieved in landscape subjects only with square or circular frames. The uneven sides of a rectangular format in a print create asymmetry. But if you strive to create symmetry within a rectangular format, it is essential to emphasize the structure and arrangement of details. Dividing lines through the middle of the picture from top to bottom and right to left can aid in this organization. Weight should be distributed evenly among the four quarters of the picture, since symmetry implies formal peace and harmony (as may exist in the representation of a round church window for example).

But perfect symmetry can be boring as well. Even in a very peaceful and symmetrical landscape, these dividing lines are often placed somewhat off center. Minimal spatial tension resulting from differing proportions is especially customary in terms of horizontal arrangement (relationships between the upper and lower halves of the picture). For example, in Photo 2, the spatial area is symmetrically divided into three equal horizontal sections. This would have produced a boring picture were it not for the horizontal lines at the top and the two at the bottom that emphasize the birch tree in the upper right-hand corner creating an imbalance. Horizontal and vertical lines drawn through the focal point—the middle of the tree—divide the picture into four quarters, in which the elements of both symmetry and asymmetry are equally represented. This is an example of one of the most frequently used patterns of formal organization found in landscape photography.

Complete symmetry is relatively rare. Is there such a thing as complete asymmetry? Probably not, since its manifestation is too variable and its evaluation very subjective. In a certain sense, complete asymmetry could be used to designate that pattern of arrangement in which the focal point bears a different relationship to each corner and each side of the picture. The focal point in the right-hand corner of an asymmetrical picture, for example, would need to be positioned so that the distance between it and each of the four corners is different for each one. The greater the difference in size, the more effective the result. Photo 7 is an example of such asymmetry.

The diagonal arrangement of a subject—generally considered an especially effective symmetrical format—can also evoke a feeling of boredom. A simple diagonal division of the picture from one corner to the other approaches symmetry and only becomes interesting when the asymmetry is accentuated, as in Photo 9, for example. Here the focal point is the diagonal placement of the boat and the extension through the boulder lying on the sand in the foreground. The subject was also asymmetrically divided horizontally in a 1:5 proportion. Interestingly enough, the horizontal line creating this division gains additional force from the boat just barely visible through the fog.

Symmetry and asymmetry are strongly influenced by color as was mentioned before. An otherwise symmetric and balanced subject can be thrown off balance with the weight of an additional color, for example, a red dot in an otherwise blue picture. The sunset in Photo 18 is a good example. The weight of the semicircular red sun dominating the right-hand side of the picture is somewhat balanced out by the shape of the lighthouse on the left. But this blue lighthouse offers only a minimal counterbalance in terms of color. In this picture, a symmetrically balanced left side is complemented by an asymmetric right side.

Thus, the arrangement of forms in a landscape should be seen as the result of individual creative intention rather than as chance. It is not a mere whim that determines the essential quality of the picture. It is good to keep this in mind for everything you photograph.

CAMERAS AND LENSES

Landscapes can be photographed with one of the modern pocket cameras. However, the resulting pictures are then destined for photo albums or wallets. An acceptable 5 × 7 inch (13 × 18 cm) enlargement of these pictures is rare.

A landscape photo intended to hang on the wall should be at least 9½ × 12 inches (24 × 30 cm). Enlarging the 12 × 17 mm mini negative is quite problematic. Even for slide projection, these pocket-size cameras produce photos with definite limitations.

Which camera then is the best one? Color landscape photography is primarily the realm of 35 mm and slide cameras. Slide photography is dominated by the classic 24 × 36 mm format. All the examples in this book were taken with 35 mm cameras, and 90 percent were printed from color slides. Slide photographers have gained recognition in the eyes of the public ever since the discovery of the technique for producing prints from slides. For enlargements to 12 × 16 or 20 × 24 inches (30 × 40 or 50 × 60 cm), however, a technically superior color negative film is required for satisfactory quality.

SLR Cameras. Two different types of cameras can be used for 35 mm photography: those with built-in rangefinders, and reflex cameras. Apertures can be manually controlled on cameras with built-in rangefinders. Unfortunately, there are only a few such cameras that fulfill the second prerequisite, namely the capability of using lenses of various focal lengths. So it is no wonder that more and more people are turning to single-lens reflex (SLR) cameras with prism rangefinders and adjustable lenses. With these cameras, the image in the viewfinder is identical to the scene being photographed. Distance and light metering are usually taken through the lens and the photographer has complete control of the pictures, no matter which lens is used.

Most of the modern reflex cameras meter at full aperture—the aperture permitting the maximum amount of light to pass through the lens under prevailing conditions. The aperture must be set for each shot and only returns to the chosen focus when the shutter is pressed (spring aperture). Thus, the camera is immediately ready for the next shot.

To aid in visual assessment of the depth of field when the light is dim, most SLR cameras are equipped for exposure control, enabling the photographer to completely control sharpness independent of distance and aperture setting. The depth of field is also marked on the lens ring.

What other standard features should a modern SLR camera have? The Leica R3, for example, has a number of lenses available with focal lengths varying from 16 to 800 mm—24 different lenses in all. Naturally two or three are enough for a start. Three are recommended here for the budding landscape photographer: a 60 mm (normal focal length) macro lens, a 180 mm telephoto lens, and a 35 mm wide-angle lens. These three will enable you to shoot most of the landscape photographs you desire, as well as a variety of other subjects.

Light Metering. Modern SLR cameras have several interesting and intriguing features. There are often three different possibilities for metering: a reflex viewfinder (ground-glass viewing screen), a microprism collar, and a sectional view indicator. The photographer can select his or her technique according to the various lenses. The most commonly used are the microprism collar and the sectional view indicator. However, the full focusing screen has definite advantages when the object to be photographed is very near, very far, or when a telephoto lens with a long focal length is used. Light is measured by a light meter built directly into the lens. The amount of light reaching the exposed film is measured accurately. Even here there are various ways in which to meter. Either the light over the entire picture area is measured (averaging), or the light over a certain detail is spot-metered. The latter technique enables the photographer to selectively measure the light hitting a chosen detail. Another advantage of this method is that the entire motif can be metered precisely in difficult light situations, for example, the strong contrast existing in backlit scenes.

Shutter Speed and Aperture. Modern SLR cameras are often equipped with an electronically controlled shutter that automatically selects the correct exposure time after the proper aperture is set. Most of the better cameras are equipped for overriding the auto-exposure system, however, and this is an important feature. With such a provision, the photographer can select both aperture and exposure time as desired within the range of 4 sec. to 1/1000 sec. The shutter speed is marked on a ring and is manually controllable. For landscape photography, especially, the choice of both shutter speed and aperture is a necessary prerequisite for the creation of individual, expressive pictures.

Lens Focal Lengths. If the examples in this book are used as a measuring stick for good landscape photography, it is of interest to note that they were taken with lenses of varying focal lengths (from 21 to 400 mm). If this analysis is further developed, you will discover that the telephoto lens is used more often than you might imagine; it is even used for vast, extensive views. Typical examples are Photos 2, 4, 6, 8, and 23. There is a wide variety of telephoto lenses available with focal lengths of 90, 100, 135, 180, 250, and 400 mm, to mention just a few. All are well suited to landscape photography. An assortment of wide-angle lenses is available as well, in addition to the normal focal length of 50 or 60 mm. Typical wide-angle lenses are 35, 28, 24, 21, 19, and 16 mm (fisheye).

The macro lens plays a special role in landscape photography, since its 60 mm focal length is well suited to a number of different subjects, from vast landscapes to extreme close-ups (flowers with a reproduction ratio of 1:1). Thus, it is one of the most widely used lenses.

The variable (zoom) lenses are next to ideal for landscape photography. They cover a definite but very limited spectrum of focal lengths. A zoom lens can often replace two or three lenses of varying focal lengths. The advantage of the zoom lens lies not so much in the blurred effect that can be produced, but rather in the adjustability of focal lengths: The photographer can catch a motif in the viewfinder exactly as desired without having to change position.

Determining the focal length that is best suited to a particular shot is the next problem. When is a wide-angle lens called for and when a telephoto? The shorter the focal length is, the larger the area recorded by the lens. For example, a focal length of 35 mm has a 64-degree angle of acceptance, while a 21 mm lens takes in an angle of 92 degrees. The 90 mm telephoto lens has a 27-degree angle of acceptance, and the 250 mm telephoto lens captures only a 10-degree angle. To use a graphic illustration, imagine the landscape as a large cake from which you are going to cut pieces of varying sizes (the viewfinder of the camera is positioned at the center of the cake). If you want a large piece, you choose the wide-angle lens; if you want to record a smaller section—a detail in the landscape perhaps—then you select the telephoto lens.

But it is not only the angle of acceptance that changes with different focal lengths; depth of field varies as well. The shorter the focal length, the larger the area that is clear and distinct. The depth of field can be read from the appropriate ring on the lens or controlled through the viewfinder (with the aperture correctly set). Practice has shown that a wide-angle lens is better suited for extensive landscapes, whereas a telephoto is best suited for specific details, as a comparison of Photos 2 and 3 clearly shows. Photo 2 was taken with a 200 mm lens, which captures a 12-degree angle of acceptance; while Photo 3 was taken with a wide-angle lens (35 mm), which takes in a 64-degree angle of acceptance. The clarity of the details in the foreground as well as in the background for both shots is due to the distance from the subject rather than to the focal length selected. In addition, the photographer took the wide-angle shot (Photo 3) at an aperture of *f*/4, whereas the telephoto shot (Photo 2) was taken at an aperture of *f*/11. The aperture setting influences depth of field as discussed above.

Everything works together: the aperture setting, the focal length, and the angle of acceptance. The aperture determines depth of field and influences the composition of the picture. Of equal importance is the selection of the shutter speed. The correct speed of a film also plays a decisive role in the selection of the shutter speed and the aperture. Light sensitivity varies from film to film and is calibrated in either ASA (American Standards Association) or DIN (German Standards Organization) values. Since this is also important for metering light, the camera must be set accordingly.

2

The Patterned or Striped Landscape

COLOR AS A GRAPHIC ELEMENT

Photographers call the kind of "bird's eye view" images that look as though they were shot from an airplane "patterned or striped landscapes." Color and form are of utmost importance in these pictures and should be selected according to the rules of color harmony and geometric order. Dissonance plays an important role here as well, for it disturbs harmony and brings an element of asymmetry into the picture. Most of the photos in this book are examples of this type of dissonance. Relationships and the interplay of form and color are discussed in the description of each photo.

Many books have been written on this subject and may be of help to those interested in exploring this topic further. Even Goethe worked out a theory of color, and his thesis is still being discussed, substantiated, and contradicted today. This is indeed an intriguing field of knowledge and its importance extends beyond the limits of natural science, beyond a discussion of the colors of light and matter, and beyond what may have once been taught in high school about the complementary colors or additive and subtractive color mixtures. These theories are primarily of interest when they constitute an obstacle in terms of the realization of certain motifs, or when they can offer help in terms of practical color composition. Generally speaking, intuition carries more weight than theory, and people photograph what they like, even if it goes against the rules.

Back to the patterned and striped landscapes. The decisive factor in these landscape shots is the interaction between form and color. Just as with the selection of new curtains for a living room, the first step is choosing a subject that is pleasing. Although you cannot alter the pattern printed on the curtains, you do have the option of varying your subject in landscape photography. You can change the position from which the shot is taken, experiment with different lenses and focal lengths, or choose to print only part of your actual shot. Varying light conditions are also an important creative element. The weather has a profound influence on the mood of a landscape. On a sunny day, for example, the zones of light and shadow bring the elements of form into sharper contrast and intensify the colors. Haze and fog, on the other hand, soften the contrasts.

The geometric elements should be clearly defined and fairly simple in patterned or striped landscape shots. The *stripes* should be broad bands of distinctive colors running horizontally, vertically, or diagonally across the picture. Other simple geometric shapes (triangles, squares, rectangles, and ovals) can be used for accent. Good examples are Photos 1–5 and the cover photo. The character of the picture is determined by the texture and color of the vegetation, the different crops being cultivated (for example, freshly plowed fields and meadows with yellow dandelions), as well as by the focal points (trees, cottages, and cliffs) and the distinctive separating lines (rivers, paths, and fences). These lines make a decisive contribution to the character of the picture by creating, increasing, or decreasing the spatial and linear relationships between objects. The photographer's job is more difficult than the artist's because he or she does not have the freedom to simply omit whatever disturbs an artistic concept. A tree cannot be felled nor can a bush be uprooted merely because they block the view or mar the shot. The amateur striving for perfect motifs will soon recognize that the patterned landscape is no easy task. But you can learn important principles of color landscape photography as well as gain practical experience useful in other branches of photography.

3
Sunsets

Contemporary poets and painters have a difficult time with the subject of sunsets. There have been too many songs about "the golden evening sun," and too often it has been depicted in water color, oil, or "supercolor." There are some photographers, too, who maintain that sunsets are plain kitsch, and they mean it, too. But can beauty in nature really be kitsch? This is not merely a question of the philosophical attitude of snobs. Even if sunsets have been painted and photographed a million times, their appeal has not diminished and they continue to be photogenic, as well as being a challenge to photographers.

Goethe studied colors and described sunsets in his *Farbenlehre* (Theory of Color) as a phenomenon of the transition of white sunlight into glowing red, which was then interpreted as the summation of dimming processes caused by atmospheric layers. This can be demonstrated by simply holding several dozen sheets of parchment paper in front of a slide projector and observing how each additional sheet increases the density of the paper, making it less transparent and causing the light on the screen to change from white to pink, to a rich orange, to deep red, and then to violet.

A similar effect recently took place at a modern Diarama show. The various phases of a sunset were demonstrated by superimposing several slides in succession, and a beautiful quick-motion sunset was simulated by fading in and out. The audience actually witnessed a sunset in the classroom, and their spontaneous exclamation of approval rewarded the lecturer for his clever idea. This rather simple technique, which has been perfected from screen and television, produces an astonishing effect. Needless to say, a sunset belongs in every slide show if the subject is landscape photography. As was pointed out in the introduction, the rich golden red appeals to our sense of color in a special way. It would be arrogant to look down on a motif that is often photographed by amateurs simply because of its popularity.

The fact that a whole chapter is devoted to this subject is of course no coincidence, though the primary intention is not to interest as many amateur photographers as possible in sunsets. This subject was selected for a different reason: In spite of their popularity, sunsets seem to pose considerable technical problems for many amateurs. But once the amateur photographer has learned to handle these problems, he or she will automatically be able to master similar difficult lighting problems.

SUNSET OR SUNRISE?

The game is the same, only it moves in different directions: Either the sun rises or it sets. What is the difference to the photographer? Even seasoned pros cannot agree on this question. Some maintain there is none and it would be impossible to distinguish one from the other in a photo. And what do the photo handbooks have to say about it? The majority claim that sunrises and sunsets are the same as far as color is concerned, and the technique involved in photographing them is also the same, which is certainly true.

Sunrises and sunsets have been studied for quite a long time and there are indeed certain differences in coloring. For example, a certain type of turquoise was visible on several early mornings following very dewy nights, though this color was never seen in the evening. It seems that the colors in the early morning are softer and more translucent.

This can be especially well studied and compared in the Scandinavian countries around the time of the midnight sun, when the sun sets and rises within the span of half an hour. However, it was difficult, if not impossible, to distinguish colors afterward in the photo. The change in color on a film conceived for medium daylight conditions, psychological attitudes, and the capacity to remember often seem to fool people.

A filter is not used for taking sunsets in general. Although the color temperature of daylight during sunset may go down as low as 2200 degrees Kelvin (K), as compared with 5600 K in the middle of the day, conversion filters, or even filters used with tungsten film calibrated for 3200 K, are used only under exceptional lighting conditions. The reason for this is clear: It is exactly the emphasis on the warm colors between orange and purple that makes for a beautiful sunset.

When a scene measuring 3800 K is taken on a daylight film of 5600 K, the warm colors are further intensified. It is not only the prevalence of red and orange that makes sunsets spectacular. The range of colors—from gleaming gold to the last reddish-purple hues—is immense.

But colors are more than an aesthetic experience for the eyes. The range of colors and form chosen by the photographer transmits strong emotions. Sunsets may be romantic, sentimental, lovely, overwhelming, or dramatic. It is the photographer who—consciously or unconsciously—incorporates his or her own personal associations. Abounding joy or restraint, passionate expression or sensitive impression, are visible in the way a sunset is taken and speak directly to the viewer who is similarly disposed.

THE SUN IN PHOTOS

There are two ways to capture a sunset on film: Either the sun itself is part of the picture, or it is pictured indirectly as a reflection on the landscape, such as the play of light on water, ice, or snow. Most photographers prefer to have the sun directly in their viewfinder, a method that demands technical expertise—to capture the sun while it is still bright enough—and leaves relatively little room for interpretation. On the other hand, a sunset seen in reflections allows much more leeway for an individual approach and is easier to take. If the sun is part of the picture, then it dominates both in shape and color, even if it is relatively small in size (Photos 15, 17, 18, and 19). However, while indirectly setting the mood in pictures with reflections in light and color, it leaves the photographer enough freedom to play with details in a motif (Photos 14, 16, and 20).

Surface details and texture camouflaged by shadow are visible only in the form of silhouettes. Lines and shapes thus visible add dynamism to the photo. They play a special role in the contrast between light and dark areas. Photos 15, 19, and 20 are good examples of how cloud formations can be effective as an element in a sunset, especially when the shadowy shapes and edges take on their own intense coloring, such as the blackish-purple in Photo 15. Similar cloud formations can be observed rather frequently, but they are rarely noticed since they do not "blind" us as the gleaming golden tones of the sun do.

An analogy can be drawn between the photographer and the painter when it comes to sunsets. The nineteenth-century German painter Caspar David Friedrich favored evening scenes precisely because of the muted halftones produced by the late evening sun.

The evening sun hidden behind clouds and haze is especially well suited for color photography. Contrasts are softened, which is an advantage, since color film can render color contrasts only to a limited degree. Under a clear blue sky, a well-chosen detail in the foreground (in Photo 17 it is the silhouette of flowers) serves to temper the all-too-glaring intensity of the sun, which in its brightness even penetrates a relatively dense tangle of plants. The effects thus created are very unusual and add a sense of motion to this picture.

Seasoned photographers recommend photographing a sunset only when one is able to look directly into the sun without having to squint. There is something to be said for this argument, but once the sun has dropped so close to the horizon, little time remains for shooting pictures. If you succeed in taking two or three really good photos within this decisive phase, you are really lucky.

METERING SUNLIGHT

No given method automatically produces satisfactory results; you have to experiment and see what happens. This advice is as old as the first manuals on color photography dealing with sunsets, where it was suggested that satisfactory results are often achieved by focusing on the brightest area in the sky and then closing down one or two stops below the meter reading. These general rules have a certain value given normal conditions. But sunset pictures with "that special something" are very rare. For an unusual shot, everyone must gather his own experience as countless sun worshippers have done before. The best method is still to note down apertures when taking special pictures; to carefully observe the results on film, drawing one's own conclusions; and then to apply the experience later when similar lighting conditions recur.

Low Contrast. When contrasts are minimal, metering light poses relatively few problems for the photographer (Photo 18). Here readings registered on the light meter generally correspond more or less to prevailing light conditions, give or take half a stop. "Late scenes" such as Photos 12 and 20 are also relatively easy to handle in terms of metering light. Here the landscape has turned into a graphic silhouette, and the aperture depends solely on the intensity of the light in the sky.

Sunlight Reflecting on Water. The reflection of sunlight on water as an additional element in the photo does not create special problems either. The light on the water is about as bright as the sky, as is clearly visible in the photo of the Arctic Ocean (Photo 13). The sun itself is discernible only as a silver reflection on the expanse of the sea bathed in gold under the evening light. This photo also provides a good example of the importance of silhouettes and shapes for the formal composition of a picture (for example, the different intensity and graphic value of shadowy regions). Normal rules for metering light should not necessarily be applied when photographing sunsets. Lighting conditions vary too widely, as can be seen by comparing the data furnished by the individual photographers for their entries.

Tripod. Working with a tripod permits longer exposure times, smaller lens openings, and thus more depth of field. In addition, it produces what photographers like to call a "starry" effect: With an aperture of *f*/16 or *f*/22, light hitting the surface of the lens is broken down so as to produce star-like beams on the photo. They usually emanate from an extremely bright point of reflection and may even be incorporated as a formal element of the composition.

Filters. So-called "special-effects filters" have recently come into fashion. These various filters are quite useful for taking sunsets. They transform light reflections into bright gleaming stars which, when a special type of filter is used, even show up as rainbow colors in a motif. In some types of photography—especially advertising—these filters have their merits, but normally such tricks diminish rather than heighten the effect of a scene.

LENS FOCAL LENGTH

In additon to exposure time, lens focal length plays an important role in sunset photography. Telephoto lenses are ideal for capturing the sun as a huge ball, but since these special lenses are relatively expensive, amateur photographers often make do with a converter. This is an optical device capable of doubling or tripling the focal length of a normal lens. Converters "eat up" an enormous amount of light, but this is relatively unimportant when working with a tripod. Since the aim is really to capture a mood when shooting sunsets, the reduction in technical/optical quality caused by the converter does not play a decisive role. Or does it? None of the photos included here was taken with a converter.

Sunset shots also call for a certain amount of telescoping. If at all possible, this should be taken into account when composing a scene. You will find out very quickly that the extent and shape of the silhouette-like outlines of a landscape determine the formal quality of a photo. Well-proportioned and successful scenes can be shot with both wide-angle and telephoto lenses. And if it is true that a sunset is more impressive the softer the color gradations and the simpler the graphical elements in the overall composition are, then H. Jürgen Neumann's photo (18) is a perfect illustration. The question of whether sunsets are actually just kitsch becomes irrelevant when looking at this picture.

4 Emotional Photography

To certain photographers, talking about *isms* such as impressionism, surrealism, and so forth, seems like trying to compete with painters and therefore is viewed with suspicion. And what about romanticism? It may be considered an intellectual approach rather than a style, for even in 1830 it was just that and nothing more. Above all, the term romanticism characterizes an emotional view of life, events, and situations—a subjective attitude toward people that has always existed and still exists. And it finds expression in photography, too.

Amateur photographers not tied by profession to any prescribed style are free to do what they like, unhampered by preconceived notions about impressionism and romanticism. As a result they often produce better pictures than many professional photographers because they do not photograph for a specific purpose but for the sheer pleasure of it. Not only are they more often ready to experiment with unconventional techniques, but they are also more honest in conveying an emotional message. Never before have amateur photographers been more creative than they are today in this age of color photography.

More than any other field of photography, landscapes offer amateur photographers the chance to forget the tried and true and give their imagination free reign. In doing so, they are not so much trying to prove themselves as photo artists, but rather they find satisfaction in expressing their own personal approach in a good photo.

PAINTERS VS. PHOTOGRAPHERS

Impressionism in painting reached its heights in the second half of the nineteenth century, coinciding with the beginning of photography. It is a small wonder then that photographers in those days were influenced by this style, and aficionados considered it a rejuvenating influence on a somewhat conventional way of seeing things. But photographers, just as painters, developed techniques that enabled them to actually depict air and light; and it is this shimmering quality that renders such unique charm to the works of impressionist painters, who were naturalists at heart.

But then painters were able to work with color, while photographers were not. They had to resort to different techniques. For example, one early master of his craft advised that all those who considered themselves artists rather than photographers always shoot their subjects slightly *out of focus* in order to avoid extreme sharpness, "which actually hurts the eye." Today, electronic cameras, the latest developments in lenses, as well as sophisticated darkroom aids, offer other and better means by which the photographer can achieve the effects of the painter. To begin with, the photographer must learn to overcome the compulsive desire to get every detail of the picture in sharp focus, and instead he or she must master the various techniques for achieving sharp and blurred zones simultaneously.

FOCUSING

Typical examples of this technique are the photos of the great French landscape photographer André Martin (Photos 21 and 22). His unusually emotional scenes are the result of very personal techniques, such as a preference for telephoto lenses (mainly a 400 mm lens on a 35 mm camera), which enabled him to achieve a very strong concentration in depth of field (Photo 21). Since he works mostly with unusual light situations—at dusk, in fog, haze, or rain—his pictures show very gentle colors and slight gradations in contrast. By opening the lens very wide, he is able to select sharp and blurred zones precisely and juxtapose them effectively. Sometimes Martin moves his camera slightly on the tripod, and by working with long exposure times, gets additional blurred zones through the slight swaying motion of the camera.

Another method for achieving sharp and blurred zones simultaneously is to dot the landscape with strong and lively colors, as shown in Photos 23 and 24. In both cases, flowers in the foreground provide the main color effect. They are so blurred that they seem to float in the air in spite of their strong colors, even though a good imagination is required to recognize them for what they are.

This technique produces two dramatic results: added dynamism in form (color as a component of form and emphasis on the foreground), and strong intensification of the overall color appeal. Photo 23 is characterized by the daring juxtaposition of blue and orange—two complementary colors—resulting in the well-known simultaneous contrast, that is, the confrontation of two diametrically opposed colors. Photo 24 exemplifies the contrast between bright and dark, color and form, between large flowers in the foreground and small ones on the water. The light pink blossoms against a dark blue background somehow produce the effect of a negative. The mood of the photographer, his emotions, and his psychological-optical reaction to nature at the moment when he released the shutter are captured in these pictures.

These photos show what the human retina would register provided it were able to focus in absolute stillness on a specific point in the landscape—a physical feat that is supposedly only possible with the aid of drugs. Normally the eye moves continually in a kind of vibrating motion when trying to focus on an object. If it could not do this, our optical nerves would register only 10 percent of our field of vision in focus. It is the optical memory—the brain—that pieces the countless optical impressions together like a mosaic and produces sharp vision as we know it.

A photographer trying to record a single disconnected impression registered by the human eye does not really transfigure a motif but rather tries to select one particular optical impression, imitating the functioning of the human eye (the picture perceived by the human retina has very little depth of field, by the way). You can test this by focusing at a point in the distance and squinting your eyes slightly; soon you will notice how the landscape seems to vibrate.

INNER AND OUTER VISION

There is another, more psychological problem involved in viewing such impressionist-like photos: the difference in individual sensitivity. A photo that normally renders reality as we see it—imperfectly—is transformed into something new by the vision and subsequent interpretation of the photographer; in its heightened aesthetic appeal, the resulting photo sometimes even surprises the photographer.

Experience shows that not only is it important to master exposure technique but that darkroom work can also be an added tool with which to achieve a photo that conveys your personal experience of a motif or subject. If a photographer can evoke an emotion similar to his or her own from an objective viewer who is able through experience to also judge the aesthetic merits of a picture, then the photographer may consider the photo a success.

The question of whether to try for painterly effects, such as R. Auer's "Rainy Day" (Photo 26), will always remain a question of the intensity of one's own experience. Technical quality, or the fun of experimenting alone, does not justify manipulation. This explains why the dividing line between painting and photography is sometimes very narrow; so narrow, in fact, that when looking at Auer's picture, an uninitiated reader might take it for the photograph of a watercolor. The detailed technical data on page 110 demonstrate how difficult it may be to capture a technically perfect impression in a photo. Needless to say, this is due less to the technical aspect of it than to the creative criteria applied and the intensity in reacting to nature. In short it is the thought behind the picture that makes it good.

As has been noted, the atmosphere can play an important role in color photography and it becomes especially effective where light and its different manifestations are included in the photo as an integral element of form. Naturally, exposure is more tricky in such cases because one is dealing with difficult and unusual lighting conditions, as the color contrast in Photos 27 and 28 shows: The colors run the complete range from the intense black of the rocks to the pure white of the sun-drenched clouds and the foaming water. Here the capacity of the lens and the film for rendering contrast is of major importance, and an excellent lens as well as superior color film are well worth the investment.

Certain compromises must be made regarding exposure time, because the photographer normally works without a contrast-balancing filter (unlike black-and-white photography, where yellow filters are often used, for example). This often results in underexposing dark zones, since the aim is to retain the light effects in the brighter areas. Or the reverse may occur: The light spots may be dimmed because the texture and detail of the darker areas are still visible (rocks in Photo 28). This is where the merits of a selective exposure meter come into play, especially when shooting against the source of light. It enables the photographer to precisely meter the light of the various details in the photo and then compute the apertures that are best suited to balance out extremes. When in doubt, one should always slightly underexpose when taking transparencies, especially when a print is desired later on. The seasoned photographer makes sure to get the desired effect by shooting the motif with various apertures.

ROMANTIC PHOTOS

Romanticism—does it still exist? Of course it does. To be a romantic means that inner vision generates intensified emotions, not to mention a strong reaction to nature. It is left up to the reader to decide where genuine feeling ends and excessive emotionalism begins. Our unemotional and prosaic world has produced a new kind of romanticism that manifests itself in an exaggerated rendition of visual experience, sometimes in sentimental emphasis of emotions, or even kitschy and false transfiguration.

The photographic version of modern romanticism can be seen in Photos 29 and 30. These are very fine examples of a subjective experience that speaks directly to the viewer. Nothing here seems exaggerated or overly emotional. The creative and interpretative approach is of special interest here. The photographer who took Photo 29, for instance, played the role of an impartial observer. He used a 200 mm lens in order to penetrate the tangle of leaves in the foreground while taking good care that his "cover" was still visible, even if only as an indefinable web of lines. The binocular-like effect emphasizes the impartiality of the observer and transmits itself to the viewer without turning him or her into a voyeur.

Strong emotions are at play in Photo 30. It conveys a feeling of being caught up in the private thoughts of the photographer. The use of a wide-angle lens successfully brings out the feeling of introspection and deep emotion in this fantastic scene, while creating a more spacious impression of this dream landscape from a surrealist fairy-tale world at the same time. Few are able to discover such a scene and only a handful can translate it into such creative photography.

The intensity and composition of painterly effects achieved by incorporating more or less blurred details, especially richly colored ones, can be easily controlled with the help of the viewfinder. More difficult are blurred effects attained with a zoom lens, or by moving the camera during exposure, though some photographers claim to master this technique to such a degree that they are able to achieve the desired result on the first try. Experience shows, however, that coincidence plays a major role here and should always be a factor in calculation. There is no doubt, however, that practicing this technique increases confidence in handling it. But the main prerequisite is a clear idea of what the final product should look like and what it should convey. In this respect the photographer, as well as the painter, begins with the same premise: Both need a definite idea of what they want to express before starting to work.

This is also true of effects attained by changing focal length with a zoom lens during exposure. Effects such as shown in Photo 48 can be varied in many ways. But working with a zoom lens when dealing with landscape photography is advisable only when it helps to convey a very precise idea more creatively; that is, only when the photographer is the absolute master of his or her equipment and can concentrate on the creative realization of the intended concept.

5

Snow and Ice—Form and Color

Colored snow—is there such a thing? Of course not. Yet watching the snow change color during the course of the day and trying to capture its changing hues is one of the most interesting challenges of modern landscape photography. Winter landscapes used to be the realm of black-and-white photographers, who tried to depict ice and snow in all their glistening glory by making full use of technical as well as artistic know-how. Graphic black-and-white photos shot against the light in order to bring out as much contrast as possible and printed on extra-hard, high-contrast paper are still considered the realm of leading amateur photographers. Unfortunately, the snow too often turns out looking like concrete, and the pictures become a rather dull symphony in gray. Color film, on the other hand, captures the lovely blue cast of the snow, as in the beautiful shot Dolf Reist took of the tower of ice—Quitaraju, in Peru (Photo 32).

Many photographers try to eliminate this blue tint, since it seems unnatural. Snow is white! Still others choose to emphasize the azure tint with blue filters, which seems quite logical and acceptable. This is not at all a question of good taste, for on a sunny day, a snow-covered winter landscape—which probably provides the brightest reflecting surface for the deep blue of the sky—takes on a definite bluish tint in the sunlit areas and a deeper blue tone in the shadows. If the object is to render what the eyes really perceive, one must accept this blue rather than trying to filter it away. Many photographers have changed their minds about such issues in recent years. Today, photographers appreciate the enriching effect of these reflected tones and often attempt to use them creatively by emphasizing them or mixing them with other colors (for example, red).

MORNING AND EVENING LIGHT

Before reading any further, take a look at Photos 31–40. These examples should prove conclusively that winter landscapes are in no way "colorless" pictures. In fact, it is difficult if not impossible to take a picture that would justify the assertion that snow and ice are predominantly white or even gray. Snow and ice are not just blue, yellow, and orange but also red and violet, depending on the colors they reflect and the time of day. Some of the loveliest winter scenes can be captured in the morning or evening, when the sun's rays approach the red-violet section of the color spectrum. Winter landscape specialists love dawn—that moment in the morning when a gentle crimson blush announces the arrival of the still distant sun—and twilight, when the last violet rays linger after the sun's departure. Many impressive landscape shots can be taken just before the sky turns completely dark by using a tripod and the snow as a source of reflected light. Observe some time how the light reflected from the snow and the intensity of the direct sun struggle against one another for effect at midday, yet slowly and increasingly begin to join forces as dusk sets in.

NEUTRAL LIGHT

Although the snow may appear gray when the sky is full of dark threatening clouds, this does not mean that you should leave your camera at home on such days. On the contrary, neutral light has definite advantages when colorful details are added and used to complement the neutral tones of snow and ice. Examples of such lighting conditions are Photos 37–40. Photo 40 depicts the slightly somber mood of such a day quite realistically, whereas the ice pictures (37–39) are the results of manipulation. The photographer used a polarizing filter, which not only counteracted the reflective quality of the ice, but caused it to appear jet-black as well. Thus, the gleaming white ice crystals and snowflakes stand out very distinctly from their ebony background.

USING FILTERS

It should be emphasized that filters are not necessary for color landscape photography. The exceptions mentioned only confirm this rule. The so-called UV filter (ultraviolet-ray-absorbing filter) has lost its original function because the emulsions and antireflective coatings of modern lenses absorb most ultraviolet rays. Color film emulsions in use today have a similar effect, so these ultraviolet filters are generally used only as lens covers. A polarizing filter on the other hand can be used to attain attractive and interesting effects as the examples show. The use of such filters will be discussed later on.

SNOW—METERING LIGHT

Accurate metering of light becomes more difficult the clearer the weather is and the higher the location (alpine mountain range). You cannot solely rely on the values registered on the light meter, because of the erratic readings it provides when held up to the dazzling amount of light reflected from snow and ice piled up at the foot of a snow-covered peak. The needle will jump to the highest possible reading and come to a dead stop when it is pointed toward the brightly glistening snow. Even coupled light meters prove a viable alternative only in certain cases. The best thing to do is to meter one area very carefully. But how?

This is where a selective light meter with a narrow angle of incidence comes in handy. With such a meter, you can take a reliable measurement of any neutral gray object (a light-colored backpack, or a gray parka belonging to a member of your party). This should be an object close by and should exclude the brightness reflected from the snow. The real perfectionist gets a so-called "gray card" (remission of 16 percent of the light striking the surface, which corresponds to the calibration of the light meter). This card facilitates reliable neutral measurement no matter what the conditions may be. If you are not equipped with such metering aids, you must rely on the snow setting indicated in the instructions accompanying your film and then try to learn from experience.

It is always advisable to take two shots, varying the aperture by a half stop when shooting important subjects. At this latitude, the period of intense sunlight during the winter months is quite short—from about 10 A.M. to about 2 P.M. With diffuse light, or with an overcast sky, choosing proper apertures is less problematic.

Typical snowscapes show a narrow range of color gradations and you are wise to vary your aperture one to one-and-one-half stops beyond the recommended setting. Perhaps the technical data accompanying the pictures will provide helpful hints in this regard.

Exposure Latitude. Color films have less exposure latitude than do black-and-white films. For this reason, selecting apertures as carefully as possible is of the utmost importance. The brightest parts of a sunlit snowscape are the critical areas. The shadow details of these parts should still be distinguishable and not be "devoured"—to use a term favored by expert photographers—by sunlight that is too harsh. The angle of the sun in relation to the direction of shooting affects the intensity of contrast. Naturally light/dark contrasts increase as you move the camera from a "sun-at-your-back" position, to a "sidelight angle" shot, to an "against-the-light" situation. With the sun at your back, the rays illuminate all surfaces with relatively equal intensity. When you shoot against the light, the contrast between light and shadow is much harsher; the lines between objects may become blurred, and the surfaces reflecting light more intense. The shadows take on a deep azure tone, an indication that you are rapidly approaching the limits where color film is capable of rendering light contrasts. When shooting backlit snowscapes, it is practical experience that counts and brings optimum results.

FROSTY DETAILS

A winter landscape is not just an extensive snow-covered field glistening in the sun, or a fir forest delicately dusted with a layer of powder. There is a wealth of seemingly insignificant motifs that are often overlooked or simply never noticed.

Close-ups. Close-ups can be just as fascinating as splendid alpine glaciers. Some of the beautiful shapes produced by cold, ice, and frost are depicted in Photos 34–39. Representative of thousands of similarly lovely details, these photos should serve to focus your attention on this aspect of winter landscapes, which offers more truly colorful images than any other. And the best part is that this is a relatively unexplored field, offering new horizons to most photographers.

Lenses. Shooting technique is relatively uncomplicated with modern SLR cameras and special close-up lenses. Even though most of the photos of snow, frost, and ice shown here were taken with telephoto lenses, more and more shots are being taken with modern macro lenses having a reproduction ratio of 1:1. When depth of field is measured in terms of centimetres or even millimetres, such a lens with a focal length of 60 mm has a definite advantage over telephoto lenses with extensive depth of field, or lenses especially designed for extreme close-ups. Those who desire extreme sharpness of detail will quickly learn to appreciate the value of the macro lens.

Close Focusing. Colors in winter close-ups are more distinct, intensified, and often tend toward a monochrome coloration (Photos 35 and 36). A few simple but graphic details should be given priority, insofar as the image is not dependent on rhythmic repetition as in Photo 37. What is problematic in such pictures is the limited range of depth of field in the lens. The closer you approach the subject, the less the depth of field, which forces you to use a larger lens opening. This requires longer exposure times and the use of a tripod.

Fortunately, you can check the sharpness in your focal zone through the viewfinder with the aperture correctly set. Arrangement and formal composition in close-ups calls for sharpness of the entire subject. Thus, the photographer should choose a relatively two-dimensional motif that is characterized by a distinctive graphic design (Photos 38 and 39). Although the photographer may manipulate contrast between distinct and indistinct zones, as in Photo 36, the subject itself should be sharp and in focus as, for example, the two snail shells in this photo. Careful use of light and shadow was instrumental in attaining the desired three-dimensional presentation of the subject.

POLARIZED LIGHT

As was mentioned before, special filters are not generally necessary for winter shots. On the other hand, a polarizing filter is a definite must for close-ups and shots taken with a macro lens.

Polarized light not only completely eliminates certain reflections and mirroring effects in nature, but also causes an intensification of color. The impression registered by the eye is modified to a certain extent here. Polarizing filters deepen the blue of the sky, which in extreme cases may approach a blackish tone (Photo 41). The reduced reflection caused by polarizing filters is especially evident in pictures of highly reflective ice surfaces—Photos 37–39 are good examples of this. Where the ice is not broken by frozen air bubbles, it seems to be an evenly colored ebony surface.

Many experts use polarizing filters when taking normal landscape shots in order to intensify the color spectrum. Polarizing filters are neutral filters, that is, colorless; but they influence all colors by minimizing the penetration of ultraviolet and polarized light rays. The degree of polarization, and thus, color intensity, can be carefully controlled by rotating the filter in front of the lens. The most distinctive effects can be precisely controlled through the reflex viewfinder of your camera. You should be sure to do this before pressing the shutter. No matter what the conditions—haze, fog, or bright sun—photos can always be improved through the use of polarizing filters, for they appear more transparent. Experience will tell whether colors manipulated in this way are to your liking. Polarizing filters can also be used to intensify certain effects; for example, wherever rainbows occur because of interfering colors (bubbles trapped in a layer of ice—Photo 39).

6

"Cityscapes" and Experimentation—Aesthetics in Precision

In the summer of 1826, Joseph Nicéphore Niépce, the inventor of photography, snapped the first photo in the history of this art. The picture he captured on the tin plate revealed the courtyard and buildings of a noble country home. Prior to 1850, the Englishman William Henry Fox Talbot, acclaimed as the discoverer of the negative-positive process and the first person to produce photographs outside a darkroom, took innumerable shots—some of which were panoramas—of buildings, streets lined with tall buildings, and squares in London, Oxford, and Cambridge. Ever since that time, cityscapes have been one of the favored photographic motifs. These early cityscapes are worlds apart from our contemporary ones, and not only in terms of technical processes. Illustrated books on London, New York, Berlin, Rome, and Paris, with photos taken by the master color photographers, are proof of this.

Nowadays, city views are sold as postcards at newsstands, as black-and-white or color snapshots, as accordion-pleated series of shots, or as slides neatly packaged in cellophane. You can be fairly certain that most important cultural and architectural sights and monuments will be included here. So the amateur photographer may well ask whether it is worthwhile taking shots of the sights that have already been so thoroughly photographed by professional photographers who can take advantage of all the latest photographic refinements. The answer in a word is "yes"!

It is one thing to buy a picture postcard and something else entirely to personally contemplate the architecture of a city with the intention of photographing it. Regardless of whether your pictures are as perfect as those of the pros, they definitely reflect your vision of the city. It used to be that tourists interested in cityscapes had to travel equipped with a sketch pad. Today small, modern, portable 35 mm cameras allow you to record on film whatever your heart desires.

ADVANCES IN COLOR PHOTOGRAPHY

During the last few decades, aesthetics in precision developed for black-and-white cityscapes, giving rise to photos precisely in focus and well-balanced in form. The attempt to capture that certain atmosphere peculiar to a city was the motivating force in only a limited number of cases. The advances in color photography with its natural emphasis on qualitative precision in shooting and developing techniques have caused the emphasis to shift more toward rendering the atmosphere of a city. The technique involved in taking such photos must also be one of precision, however; perhaps even more so, since capturing a mood in a photo is both a technical as well as a creative problem. It is often only a short step from an intriguing impression to kitsch.

The pictures for this chapter were chosen for the mood they convey (Photos 40–45). Photos 46–50 also provide a stimulus for experimenting with new shooting and developing techniques, particularly those well suited to landscape photography. Use of these techniques is in part a question of preference, or rather one of experimenting with artistic and photographic techniques. Particular techniques discussed here are the zoom effect (Photos 47 and 48), sandwiching (Photo 49), solarization, and working with microscopes (Photo 51).

EQUIPMENT

The amateur landscape photographer can experiment with various creative means of arrangement, composition, and shooting. First, consider the equipment available. Naturally, experimentation requires a good assortment of lenses, particularly wide-angle lenses. The 21 mm lens (used for Photo 41) and lenses with even shorter focal lengths (for example, the 16 mm fisheye) are useful only in special cases. On the other hand, wide-angles from 28 to 35 mm are often used as are "mini" telephoto lenses, with focal lengths of 90, 135, or 180 mm. The normal lens (50–60 mm) is usually either too short or too long, as this selection of photos shows, for none was shot with a normal lens.

The major difficulty involved in using a 35 mm camera to photograph large architectural structures, such as streets lined with tall buildings or even squares, is the slanting lines that result. For this reason, the professional photographer often uses a large-format camera with an adjustable lens, which causes less distortion. Adjustable lenses are also available for 35 mm cameras (for example, the PA-Curtagon-R 35 mm *f*/4 lens for the Leica R3, which is adjustable both horizontally and vertically).

With a 35 mm camera and a fixed lens, the higher the subject is positioned, the more the walls of the buildings seem to slant (for example, when trying to capture the roof or the tip of a church tower). Since these slanting lines are not always desirable and do not necessarily add the appropriate creative or artistic touch, as in Photo 41, one must make compromises. The extent of compromise necessary is determined by the focal length, the distance from the structure being photographed, and the possibility of shooting from another, somewhat higher position. Whenever possible, the interesting architectural details of a house should be taken from across the street.

Although the wide-angle lens is most useful for shots of streets lined with tall buildings, the shorter the focal length of the lens, the more danger there is of slanting lines. When the only option is to include the strongly tapering lines, then you should do so and even emphasize them. Just be sure that the buildings do not lean either to the right or to the left. When using a longer-focal-length lens (135 mm for example, as in Photos 42 and 43), vertical lines will be straight only when the photographer stands far enough away and somewhat above the level of the street.

CREATING ATMOSPHERE WITH COLOR

There are no set rules for using color in cityscapes. In the first place, color depends not only on the subject's natural color, but also on the time of day, and the existing light conditions on the whole. Facades reflect both color and light. Strong sunlight falling at a sharp angle creates definitive zones of shadows that can be quite problematic. A slightly overcast day with plenty of sunlight is the best time to capture color cityscapes. Details in the design and tonal separation will be well reproduced, and even the delicate hues will be rendered in their true gradations under such conditions.

But effective photos can also be taken in full sunlight, as Julius Motal's photo of a metropolis shows (Photo 41). Grimly threatening, the blue-on-blue tones of the imposing New York skyscrapers seem to have been drawn with a compass, and the white sun has torn a hole in the blue of the sky; its rays create a string of magic reflections traveling across the photo. Near the edges, the sky appears black as it melts into the silhouetted facades of the steel giants—impressions of a ponderous scene—reminiscent of cityscapes created by Lionel Feininger with a brush and palette.

Diffuse light, haze, or fog can be most satisfying for the amateur photographer. Photo 43 is an excellent example of how such conditions modify a cityscape. What is important here is not the maze of signs and lights at the intersection, but rather the representation of a typical, somewhat gloomy autumn day. The motif is therefore only the vehicle for transmitting the atmosphere. Similar motifs can be found throughout the city on dark, rainy days. Such shots are usually best taken at dusk when the lights are first turned on in the houses and shops, giving new life to the gray monotony.

THE EXCEPTION: NIGHT SHOTS

The best night shots are those taken at twilight; at least that is one of the old rules of photography. Today's color films retain their full efficiency up to a sensitivity of ASA 400–800 (27–30 DIN), making this statement seem only partially correct. Of course, twilight is ideal for capturing the details of a facade, yet it is only the true night shot that can convey the actual mood of an evening scene. One should not be afraid of the harsh silhouettes that are the result of the stark contrast between the ebony of the night sky and the gleaming street lights, the brightly lit shop windows, and the glaring neon signs. The impact heightens as the contrast increases, and this is the dynamism of night shots (Photos 44–46). Haze, fog, or the smokestack of a huge industrial complex (Photo 44) dramatizes the cityscape and lends it character, be it friendly or threatening.

Rain and the brilliant color reflections in puddles on the pavement enliven the night scene. Photo 45, an exceptional photo of a thunderstorm, takes on an impressive quality through the reflections from the rainy street and from the tin roof briefly illuminated by the flash of lightning. The strands of color left by the night traffic are very important. Brightly lit buses, trams, and cars magically create attractive patterns of light in the shots taken from a tripod. The night photo of Market Street in San Francisco taken from the 25th floor of a skyscraper is a good example of this.

EXPERIMENTS—TOO MUCH SALT IN THE PHOTOGRAPHIC SOUP?

It is not the intent of this book to encourage the amateur photographer to arbitrarily experiment with different techniques. Application of these techniques presupposes an avid interest in free creation of form and color, as well as extensive experience with darkroom techniques. Photographic experiments such as those used in Photos 47–52 are by no means unusual or new, as some may think. Photo buffs have been experimenting with cameras and in darkrooms for quite a few years now. Clearly, these techniques can help train the eye and expand your knowledge of photographic technology, as well as perhaps trigger your imagination. In addition to satisfying intellectual curiosity and photo-technical creativity, these experiments can lead to the creation of photos that satisfy artistic demands. Even the amateur photographer can attain the highest level of artistic achievement possible in the art of photography.

Photos 47–52 are examples of some of the most important experimental techniques used in contemporary photography. There is one example of each technique. Sandwiching is probably used most often and involves minimal additional expense. It is a variation of double or multiple exposure but eliminates the necessity of having to expose the particular frames successively without interruption. The subjects, taken in different locations, with different film and photographic equipment, are simply mounted one on top of the other in a slide frame. Naturally, the two shots must complement each other and work together to create a new picture. Good sandwiching requires careful planning prior to shooting the individual exposures, which means that each shot is especially conceived with the idea of a sandwich in mind.

Zoom lenses were not designed solely for the purpose of creating the blurred effects that are so popular today. The ability to precisely regulate the focal length of the lens within a certain range (for example, 80–200 mm) so as to capture a subject to its best advantage is a tremendous advantage especially for landscapes and cityscapes. Yet the blurred effect attained by adjusting the focal length while exposing can still be a pleasant and interesting experimental technique. Comparing two examples (Photos 47 and 48), one can see how effective the results can be. The details of these shots are discussed in the section on technical information.

Artistic and creative accents can also be attained with solarization (Photo 49) and the use of infrared color film. However, complete mastery of shooting and darkroom reproduction techniques are absolute prerequisites for the free creation of form and color. Details of working with these techniques are discussed in Chapters 7 and 8.

7

Experimenting with Equal Densities

The invention of Agfacontour film has greatly simplified the process of density slicing. For a long time, this was viewed merely as a technique for attaining special photographic effects, offering the possibility of turning a bad photo into an interesting picture at least. The technique is the Sabattier effect, also known as pseudo-solarization. Agfacontour Professional film enables the photographer, through precise computing of technical data, to produce equal densities and to freely create interesting color compositions reflecting his or her own ideas and temperament just as a graphic artist or painter would.

DENSITY SLICING

Agfacontour Professional black-and-white negative film offers the possibility of filtering out as much blackness as desired from a black-and-white negative (or from a reprinted color film). The blackness of a black-and-white negative can be separated into density layers according to density, that is, any degree of gray can be filtered out. The result is a range of so-called "slices" of equal density or blackness (in German *Äquidensiten*). English nomenclature has given this procedure a more graphic description in "density slicing."

These segments can be sliced thick or thin, as you please; that is, you can produce narrower or wider densities by using yellow filters of varying density during the copying process. Selecting the darkest or lightest gray area is determined by choosing relevant exposure times. Exposure time depends on the brightness of the copy lamp, the distance between the source of light and the film, and the density of the yellow filter used. Exposure time is the key to determining densities. Several trial exposures with Agfacontour film will be necessary to attain the desired densities. The selected negative can be reproduced either as a contact print or as an enlargement.

Before attempting to offer precise guidelines for obtaining the darkest or lightest gray area, the goal to be kept in mind during experimentation with this technique should be pointed out. Assuming that the exposure is set for the lowest degree of blackness, you could divide the entire range of blackness into slices of equal thickness. The weakest degree of blackness (lightest part of the negative) usually corresponds to the basic emulsion of the film. If this has the value 0.3

and the densest part of the negative 1.8, then the range of blackness is 1.5. If you divide this into five equal sections of 0.3 each, then the first slice extends from 0.3 to 0.6, the second from 0.6 to 0.9, the third from 0.9 to 1.2, the fourth from 1.2 to 1.5, and the fifth from 1.5 to 1.8. When this has been accomplished, the photo is completely *densitometrized,* as the professional says.

The five slices, obtained through a five-stage copying process, are called a density group. Each individual density slice is a transparent piece of the Agfacontour film. When these five Agfacontour films are superimposed in a sort of sandwich, the picture appears completely black, as they form a completely opaque surface. If the negatives were printed onto hard lith film (the negatives would appear as positives on this film), they would again produce a completely black picture when sandwiched together. In order to distinguish the density slices from one another, varying colors can be added to the lith film. There are various methods of accomplishing this.

All photographers not well versed in this technique should copy their first density slices onto lith film, as this facilitates sandwiching. The density slices are modified through a so-called chromogenic procedure, resulting in various monochrome-colored lith films that are then sandwiched to produce a multicolored picture. With this special developing technique, the silver picture—exposed in the dark and processed in the light—is transformed into a monochrome color picture. There are about ten easily distinguishable colors from which to choose for the chromogenic developing. If the negatives are printed onto color film or color paper, however (using various color filters and color-filter densities in the enlarger), the result is an endless variety of possible modifications of color and form.

"ZEBRA" PICTURES IN COLOR

In your first attempts at superimposing various color densities, space will most probably appear between the individual slices. Should this not be to your liking, you must expand the slices by using a lower-density yellow filter in the copying process. On the other hand, should the individual slices overlap to a great extent, then the slices are too large. You can reduce the size of these slices through the use of a slightly denser yellow filter. Also, this is one way of checking whether the proper exposure time and yellow filter were used to attain the desired density of 0.3. The ideal is to have the five slices bordering each other exactly or overlapping only slightly.

Some Pointers. To simplify matters and to help you produce creative and attractive pictures, the following pointers are offered: The original negative should not be overdeveloped. The enlarger should be equipped with a 75-watt opal bulb and a 0.70 yellow filter. The accurately masked 35 mm negative should be placed in the enlarger. If the focal length is 60 mm and the aperture *f*/4.5, the format would be 4 × 5 inches (10 × 15 cm). Then three successive exposures of 4.5, 9, and 18 sec. should be made with Agfacontour film (5 × 7 inch [13 × 18 cm] format). A trial run, with a 9-sec. exposure produced the density slice that corresponded to the lowest density of the negative in the test done for this book. Since the production of a density slice depends on the density of the negative, the two alternate timings of 4.5 and 18 sec. are given in these instructions. Of the three exposures, one should produce at least one density slice. The density obtained with the shortest exposure time will become the point of departure for the production of a number of densities, that is of a range of differing slices.

Assuming that the slices of the lowest density were obtained with an exposure time of 4.5 sec., then the following pattern should be used for exposing: 4.5, 9, 18, 36, and 72 sec. In this way, you will get five equally wide density slices, which can then be copied onto lith film as described. Various colors are then added to the lith films. Please note that the film must be processed in a special Agfacontour developer and agitated constantly. (Follow the instructions in the package for use). Exposure time should be carefully noted down with the first density. You can then proceed to eliminate any degree of gray by simply varying exposure time. The Agfa-Gevaert Gevaline G 7 c developer and Gevalith Ortho RO 81 p film are used for printing the density slices prior to further processing and coloring.

In the beginning, it is advisable to make several prints of each density slice—three for example. This will enable you to add different colors with the chromogenic developer. With three density slices in three colors each at your disposal, you have a wide range of possible combinations from which to choose. Experience has shown that a black slice (simply a lith film copy of the appropriate density slice) should be used in addition to the colored density slices where emphasis is needed to bring out form. Photo 50 serves as an illustration of the results obtainable with this technique.

8 Infrared Color Photography

In landscape photography, the subjective, creative elements influence the end result considerably, as does the total change of color—the deliberate attempt at artificiality. Calling this simply and flatly "experimental photography" is not justified, however. Most people prefer to think that experiments in photography result in photos that are characterized by something unfinished, blatantly manipulated, or coincidental; while a photo that is the product of an intellectual concept and subsequent resolute realization of this concept merits consideration as a technique on a par with any other in photography. The specific photographic approach, technique, or darkroom manipulation is of little consequence when judging color, form, content, and aesthetic appeal.

The many possibilities offered by the infrared-sensitive Ektachrome infrared film—a cross between a diapositive and infrared film—has inspired the imagination of countless photographers. It was developed during the war for aerial reconnaissance missions in the United States and is widely used today in the field of science and technology, especially in forestry, hydrology, microphotography, archeology, biology, and so on.

Amateurs and professional photographers interested in creative color photography have long recognized the value offered by Ektachrome infrared film and have been inspired by its technical possibilities. It must be said, however, that only those amateurs endowed with truly creative talent are able to produce photos of artistic merit.

FILM PROPERTIES

What are the specific properties of this unusual "false-color film"? To begin with, it is a highly sensitive 35 mm diapositive film with 20 frames to one roll. It distinguishes itself from normal color film by the fact that it is not sensitized for blue, green, and red, but instead for green, red, and infrared. The infrared sensitivity lies between 700 and 900 nanometres (nm) with a maximum sensitivity ranging between 700 and 800 nm. All three colors are equally sensitive to short-wave radiation. To guarantee absorption of these waves, a strong yellow filter is generally used.

After exposure, the film reacts like a normal diapositive film while the layers sensitive to green show up as yellow, the red as purple (magenta), and the infrared as bluish-green (cyan). The photographer should keep this color transformation well in mind when looking through the viewfinder and approaching a motif. The initial results will probably prove unsatisfactory, since this technique takes some practice.

Studying the properties of the different layers, one sees how the colors change.

LAMINATION AND EFFECT OF EKTACHROME INFRARED FILM

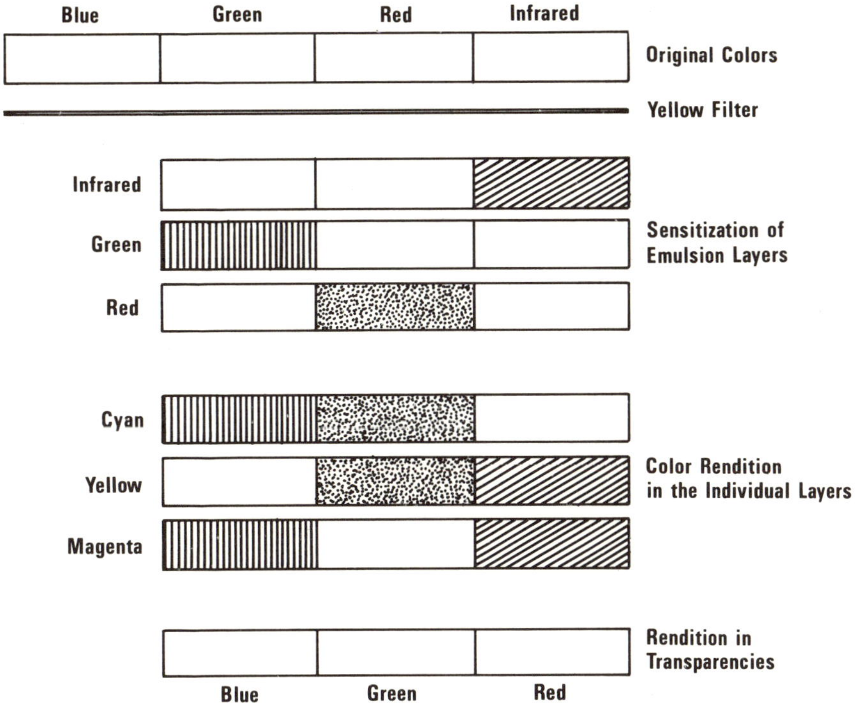

COLOR RENDITION OF EKTACHROME INFRARED FILM

Normal Color Impression	Without Infrared Absorption (Strong IR Reflection)	With Infrared Absorption (Little IR Reflection)
Blue-green (cyan)	Purple (magenta)	Blue
Purple (magenta)	Yellow	Green
Yellow	Gray or white	Blue-green (cyan)
Red	Yellow	Green
Green	Purple (magenta)	Blue
Blue	Red	Neutral (gray)
Neutral (gray)	Red	Neutral

Although the laminated colors—yellow, purple (magenta), and blue-green (cyan)—correspond to the three layers on a normal diapositive film, they deviate in reaction to their respective spectral colors, thus resulting in color images that differ from the images perceived by the eye. Color rendition depends on the amount of infrared rays registered by the film. But since only one layer is infrared-sensitized, and generally smaller lens openings are used for greater depth of field, the normally valid readings for setting focal distance on the lens (on most lenses the infrared "IR" stop) are marked on the distance meter ring. Setting your lens is especially important when working with black-and-white infrared films.

FILTERS AND INFRARED FILM

The use of various filters—except those recommended as standard filters by Kodak, such as yellow filters No. 12 or No. 15—offers additional possibilities for changing color value, the effect of which can be gauged confidently only after a certain amount of practice. The use of a polarizing filter, for instance, guarantees interesting and appealing effects, as do green, orange, and red filters.

The use of filters naturally affects the sensitivity of the film used, and this should be kept in mind when selecting apertures and shutter speeds. Since precise film sensitivity is impossible to gauge, the manufacturers give guidelines based on practical experience. "Normal" sensitivity with a Kodak No. 12 yellow filter is given with ASA 100 (21 DIN) film; if a green filter is used, it is ASA 64 (19 DIN); if an orange filter is used, it is about ASA 80 (20 DIN); and with a red filter, it is about ASA 25 (15 DIN). Newcomers in the field should experiment with various apertures and speeds, note down the data, and carefully compare the results.

EXPOSURE OF INFRARED FILM

Another note of caution: When exposing Ektachrome infrared film, you should try not to expose longer than 1/30 sec., since difficult-to-control color deviations will result. When exposing at 1/10 sec., for instance, the lens would have to be opened by one additional stop and deviation in color would have to be compensated for with a Kodak CC 20 B filter. The leeway in exposure is only plus or minus ½ lens stop, indicating the absolute necessity of accurate exposure if satisfactory results are expected. Any commercial color lab that handles Ektachrome film is able to develop such films. Individuals with some experience in developing can process their film in utter darkness themselves. Exposed film should be developed quickly; unexposed material should be stored in a cool place at a maximum of 54 F (12 C). Films stored longer than 6 months only last if they have been stored in their original package in a refrigerator at temperatures between 2 and −11 F (−19 and −24 C).

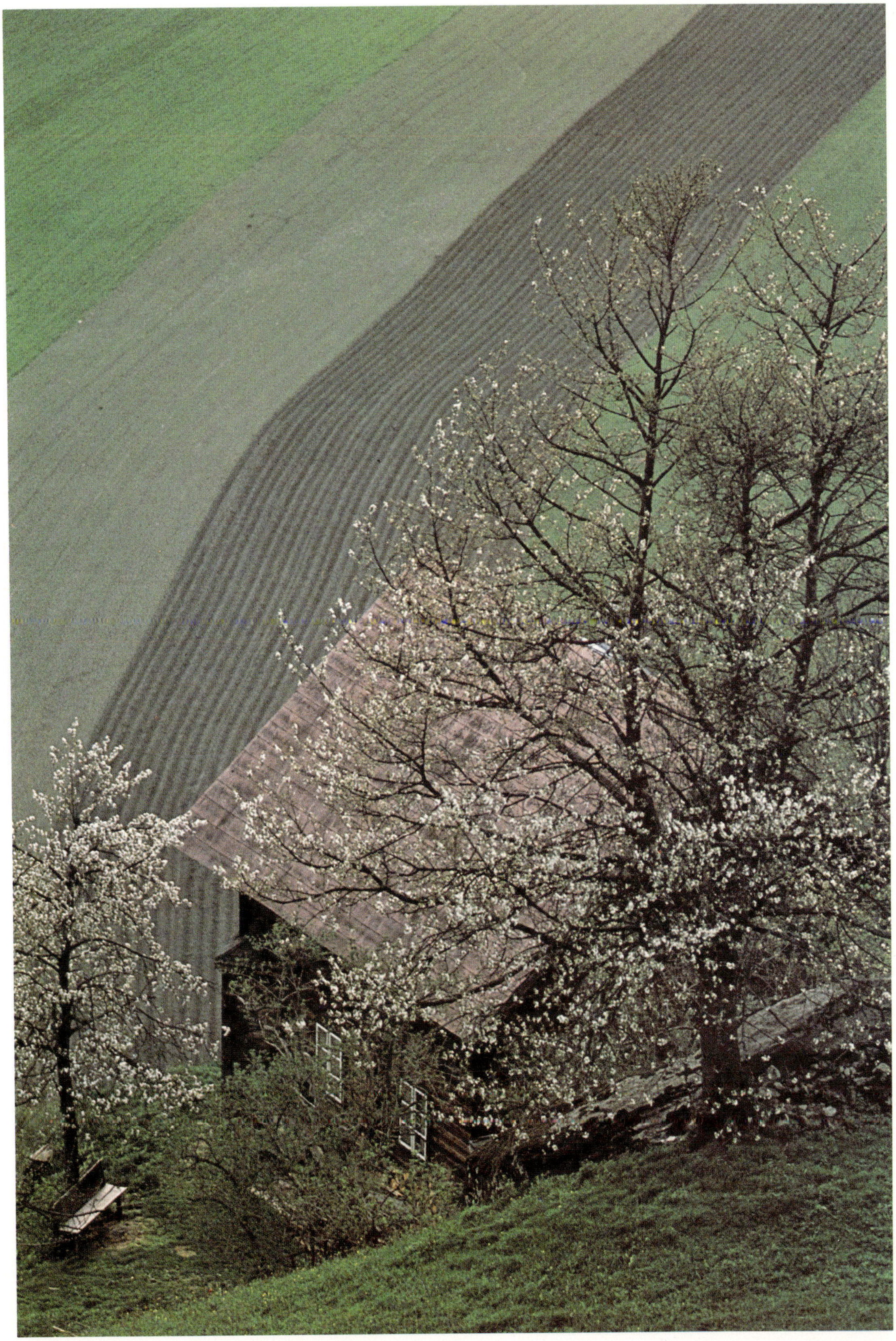

1

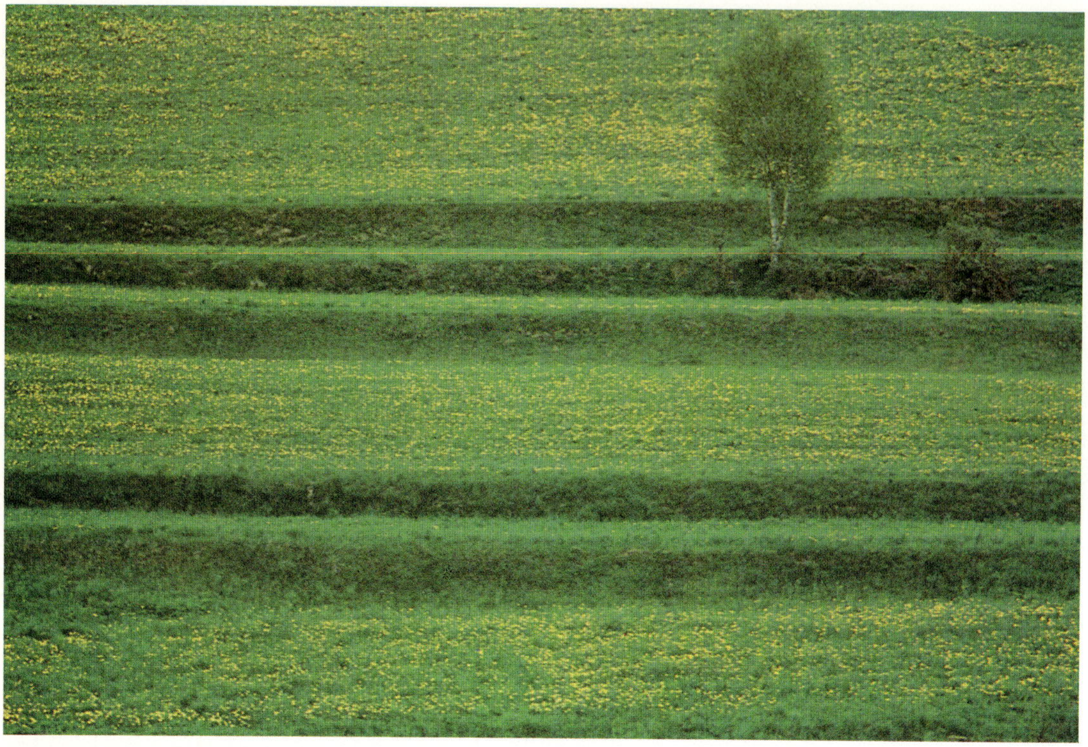

2

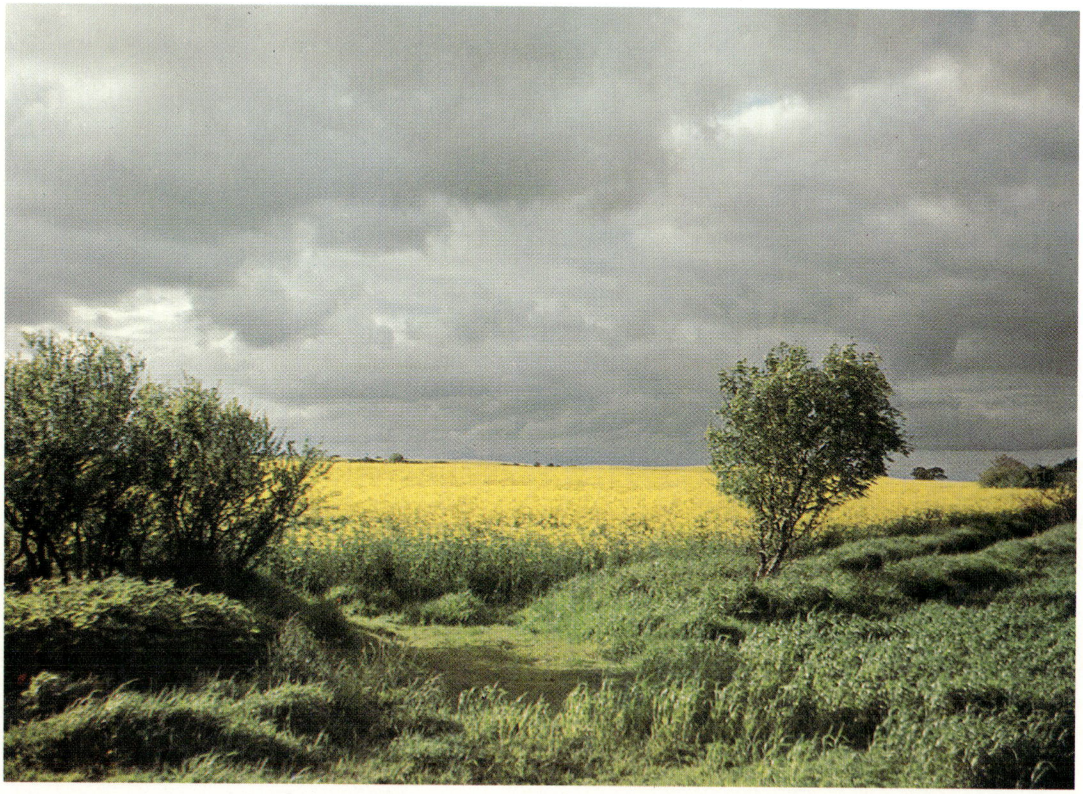

3

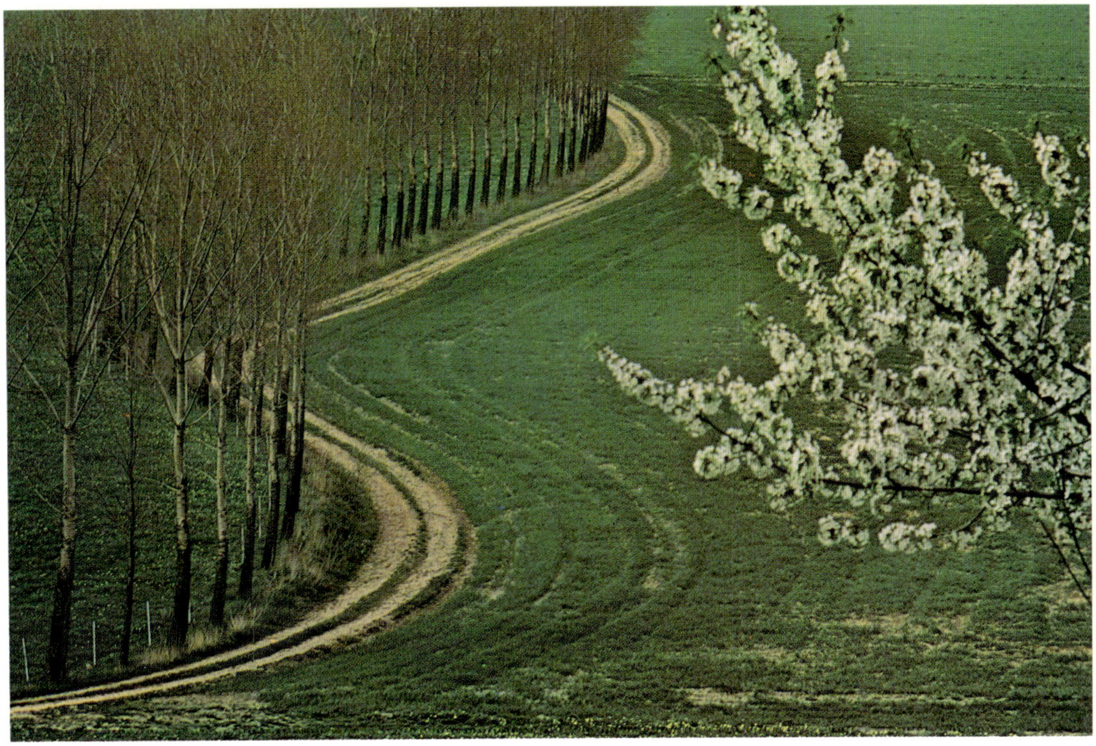

4

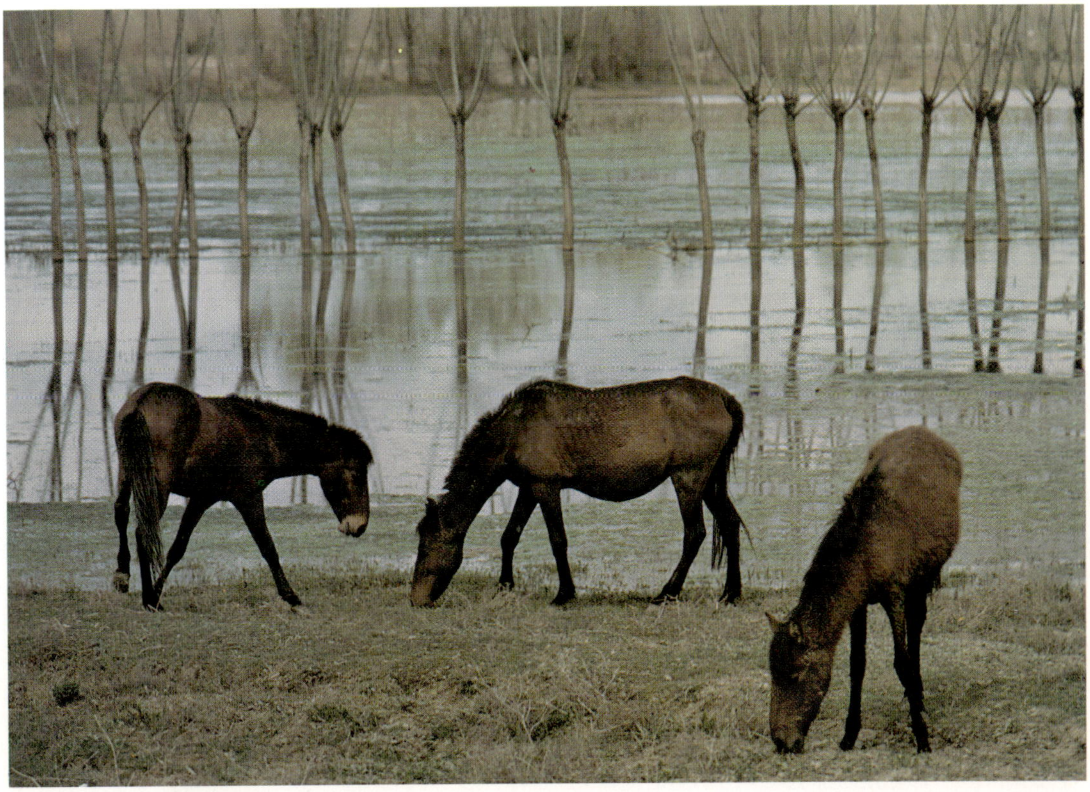

5

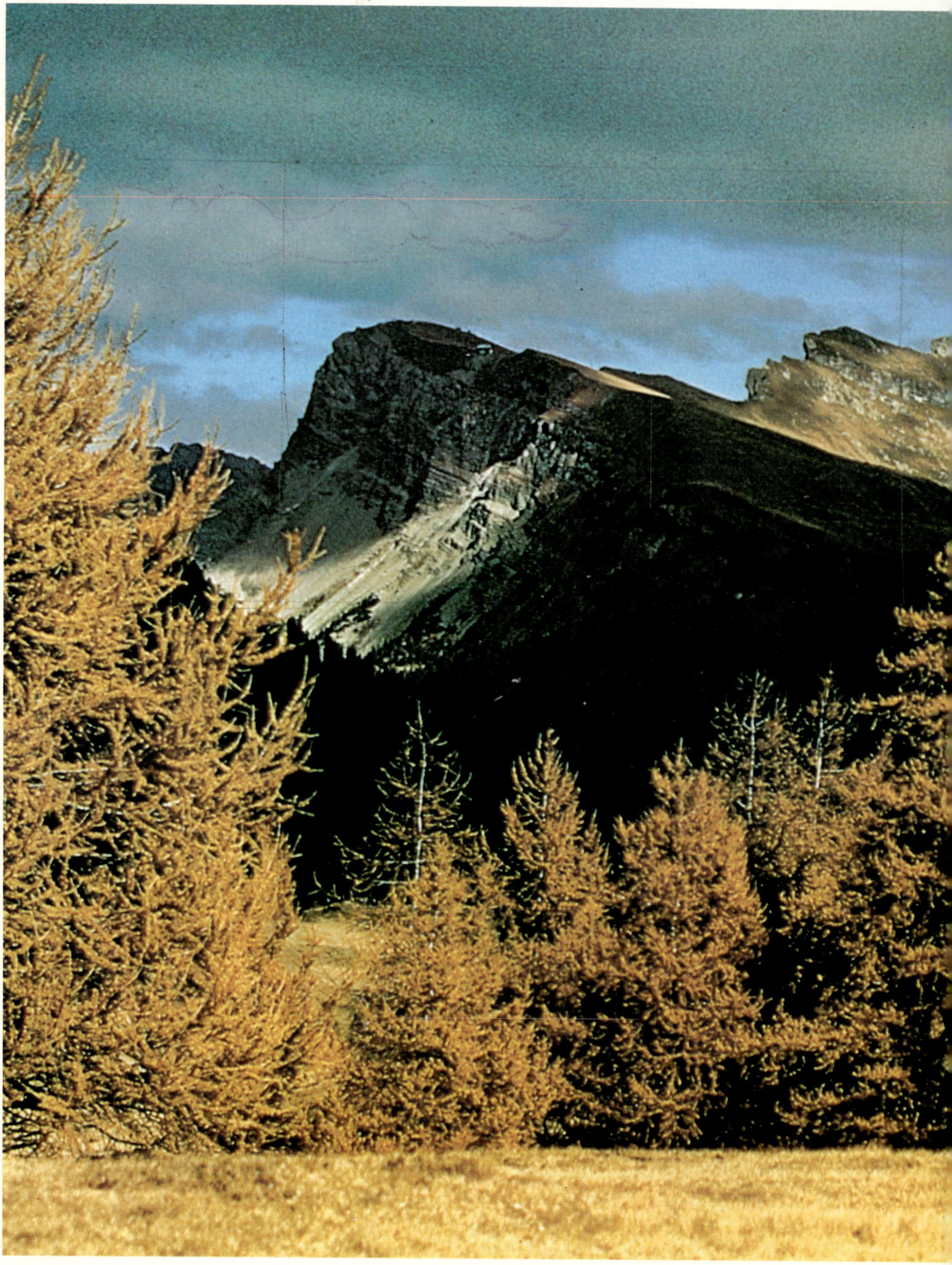

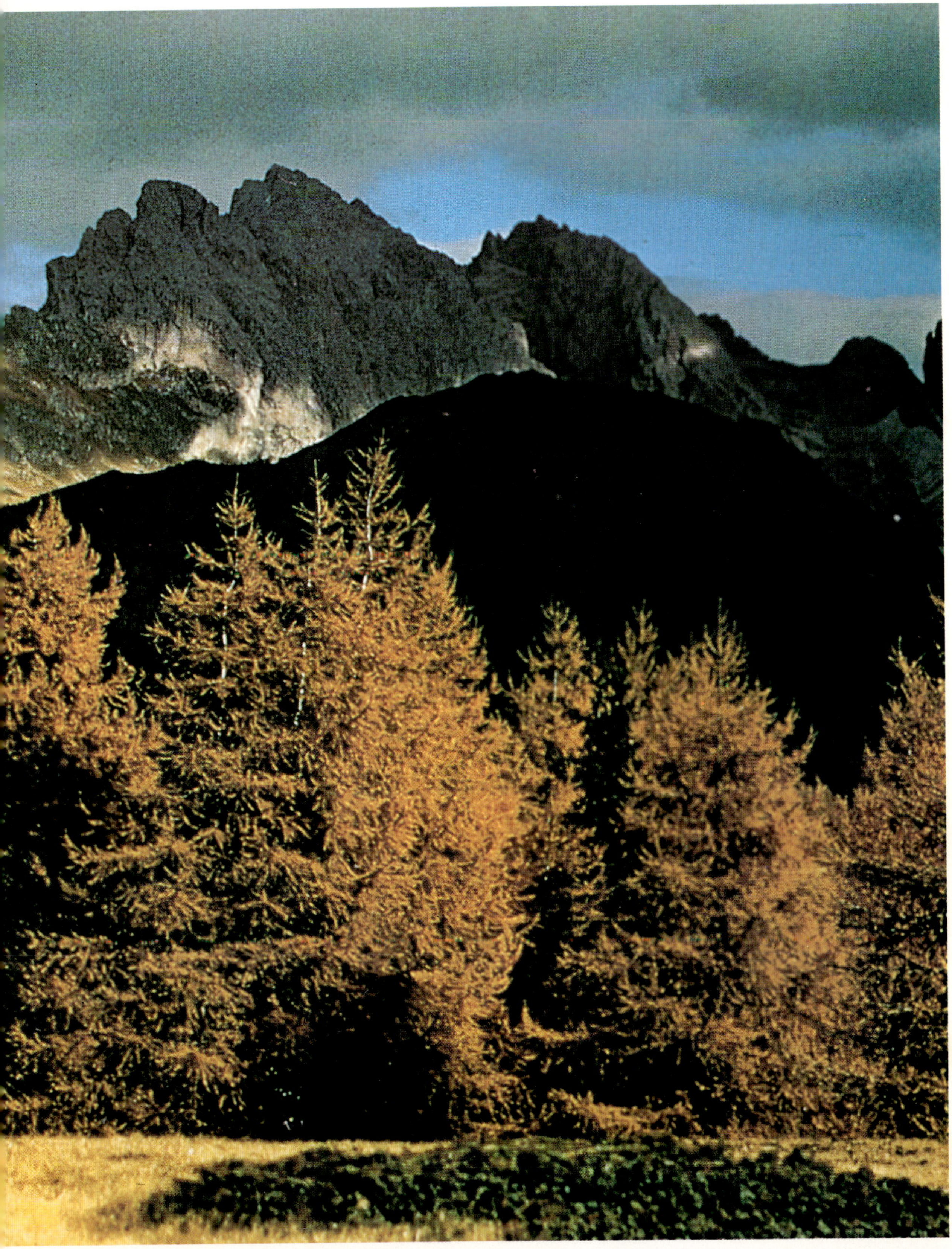

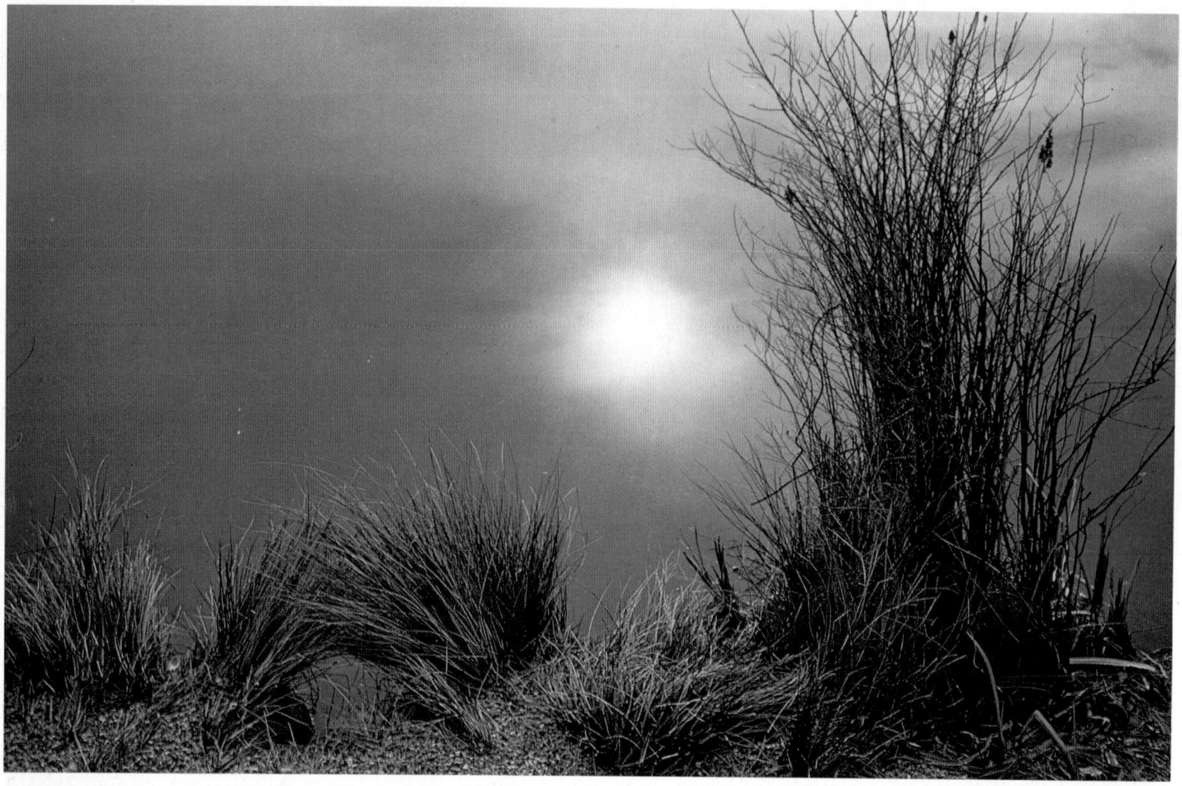
7

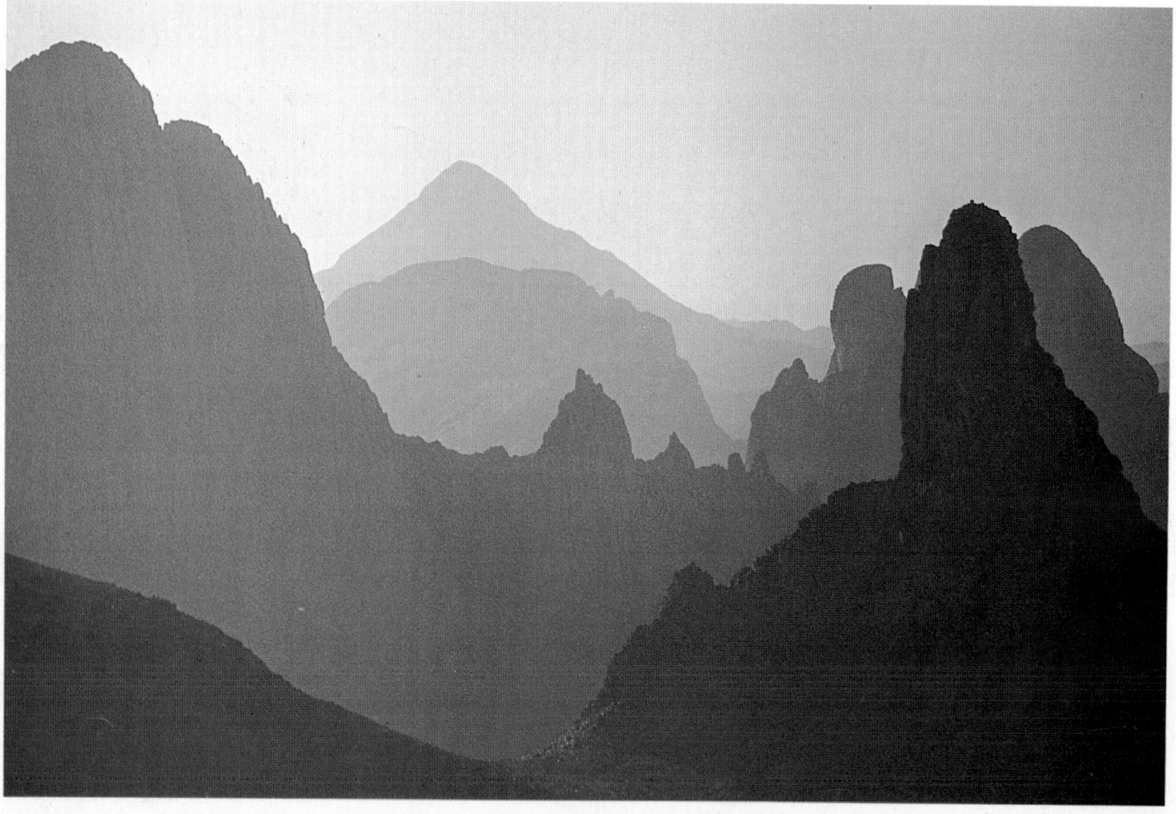
8

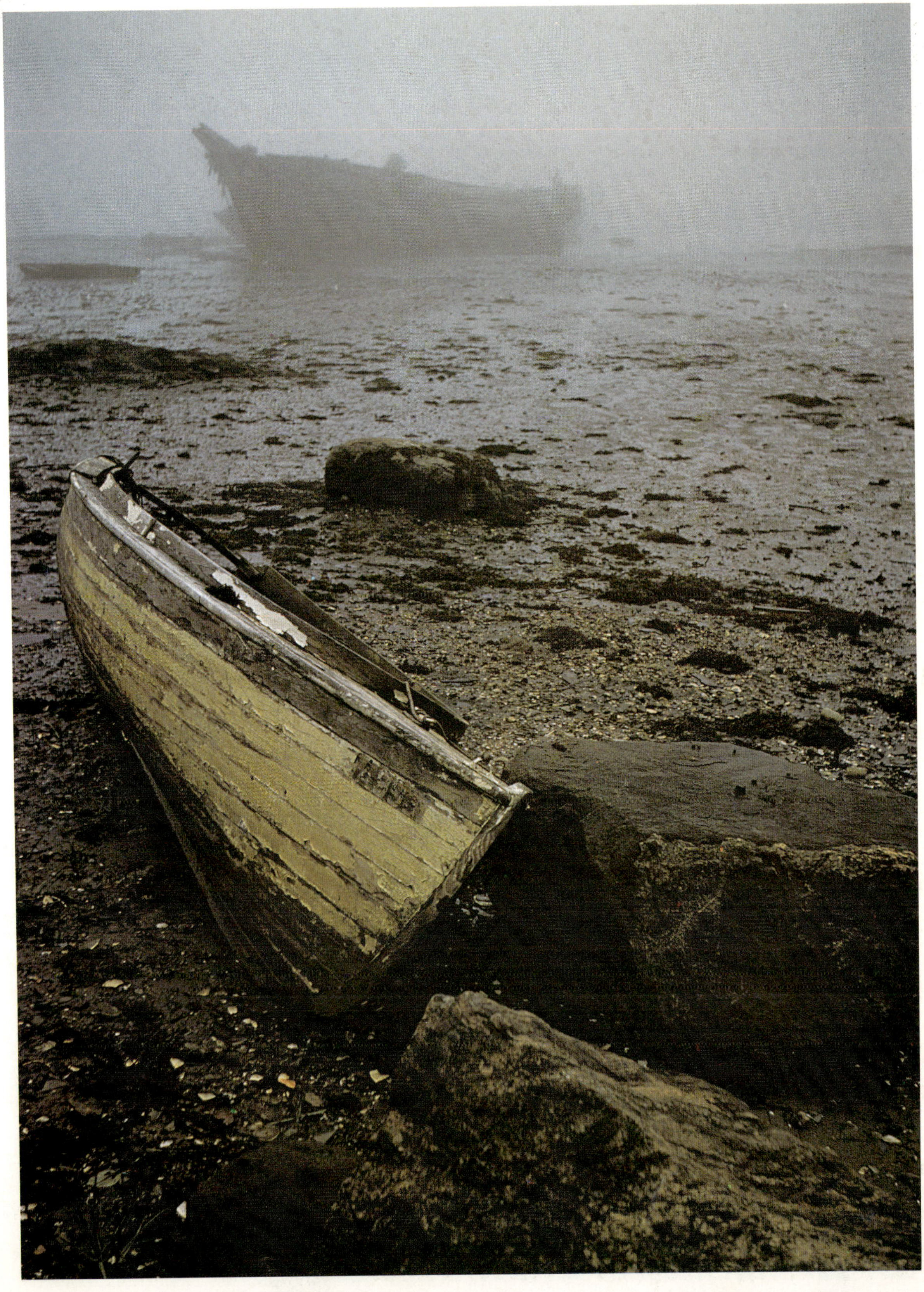

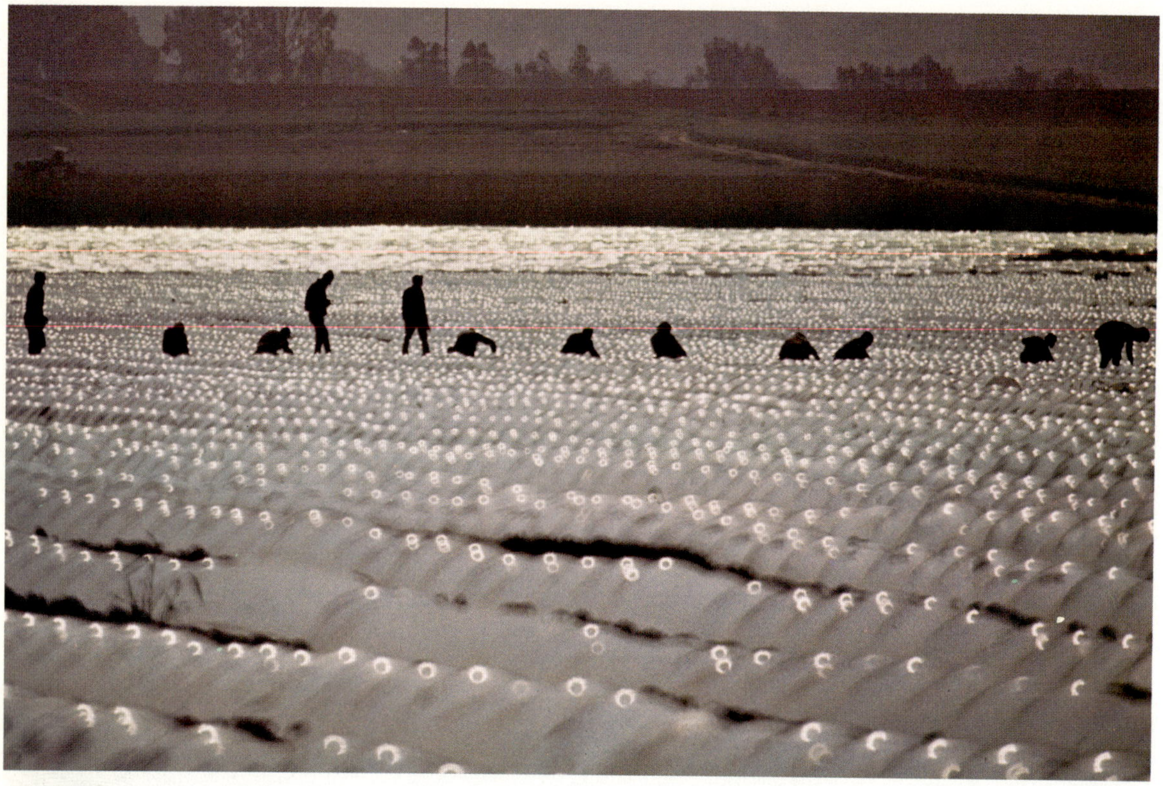

10

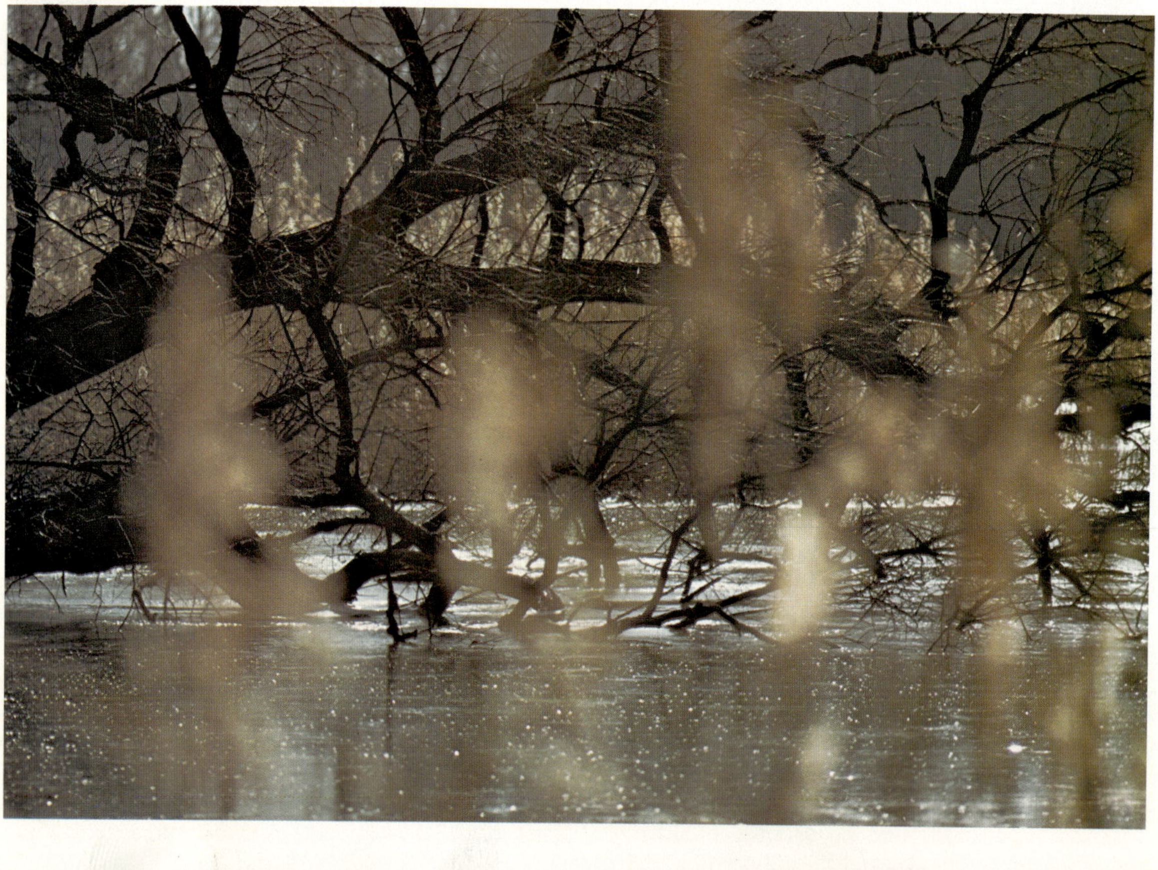

11

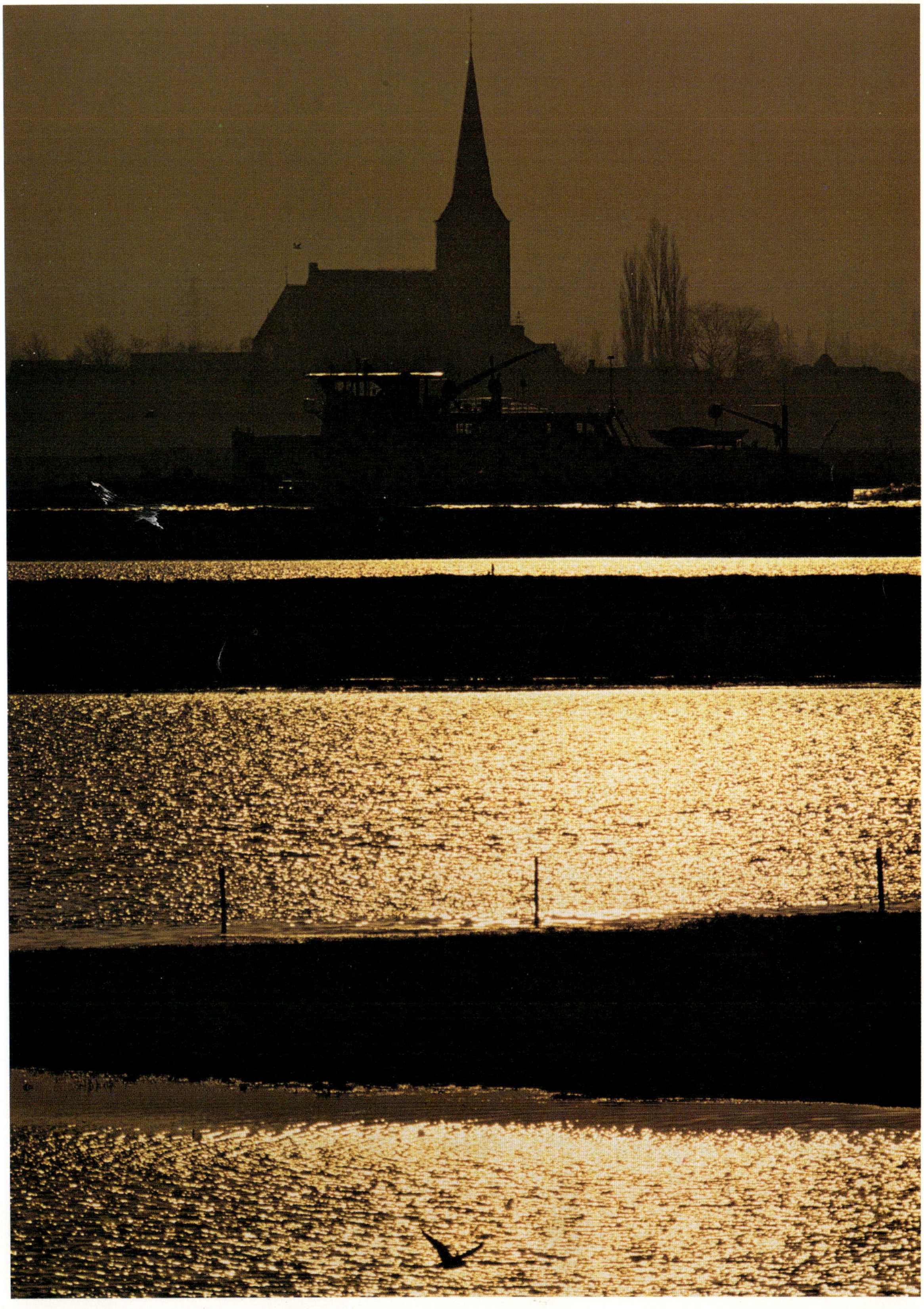

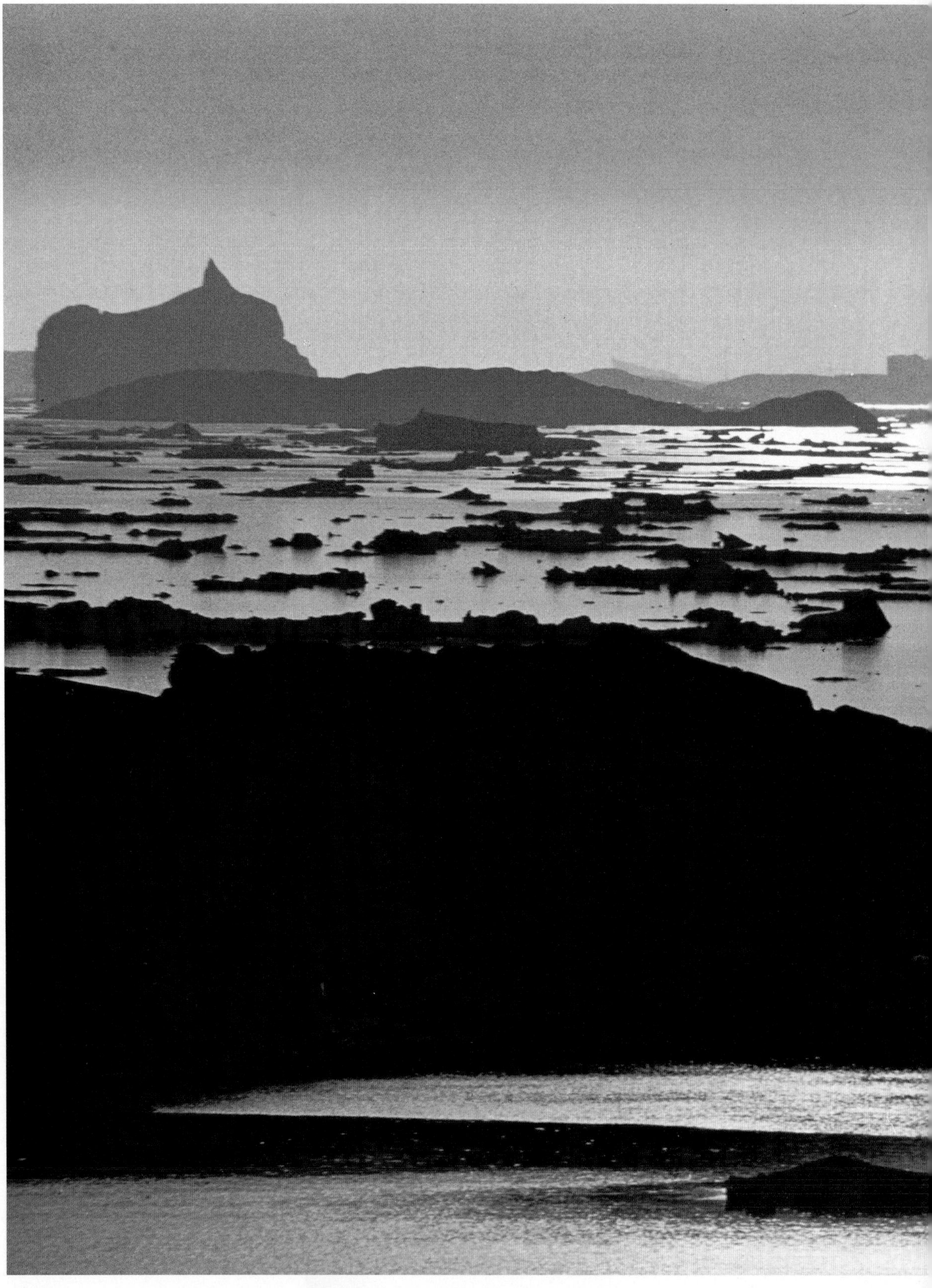

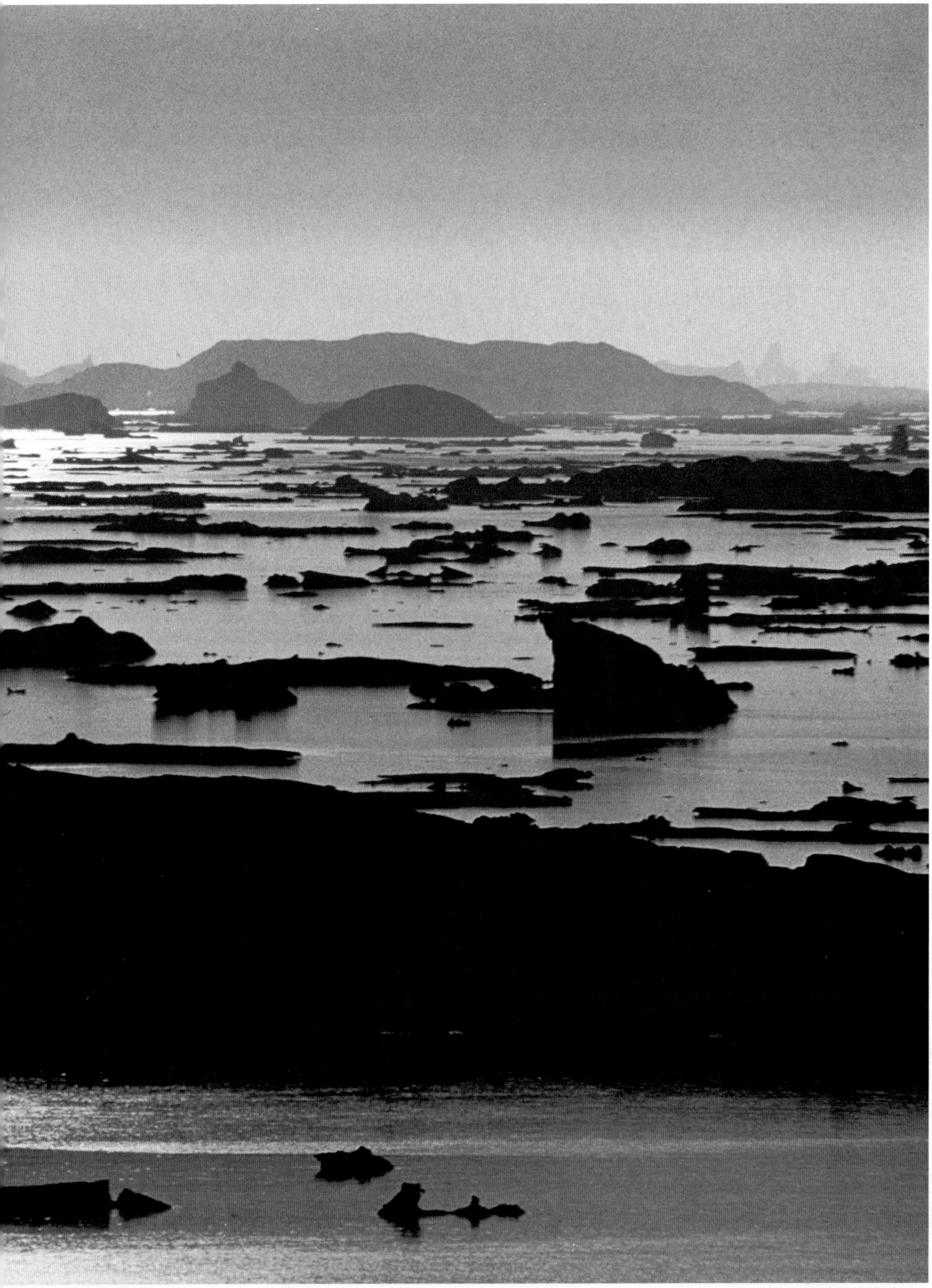

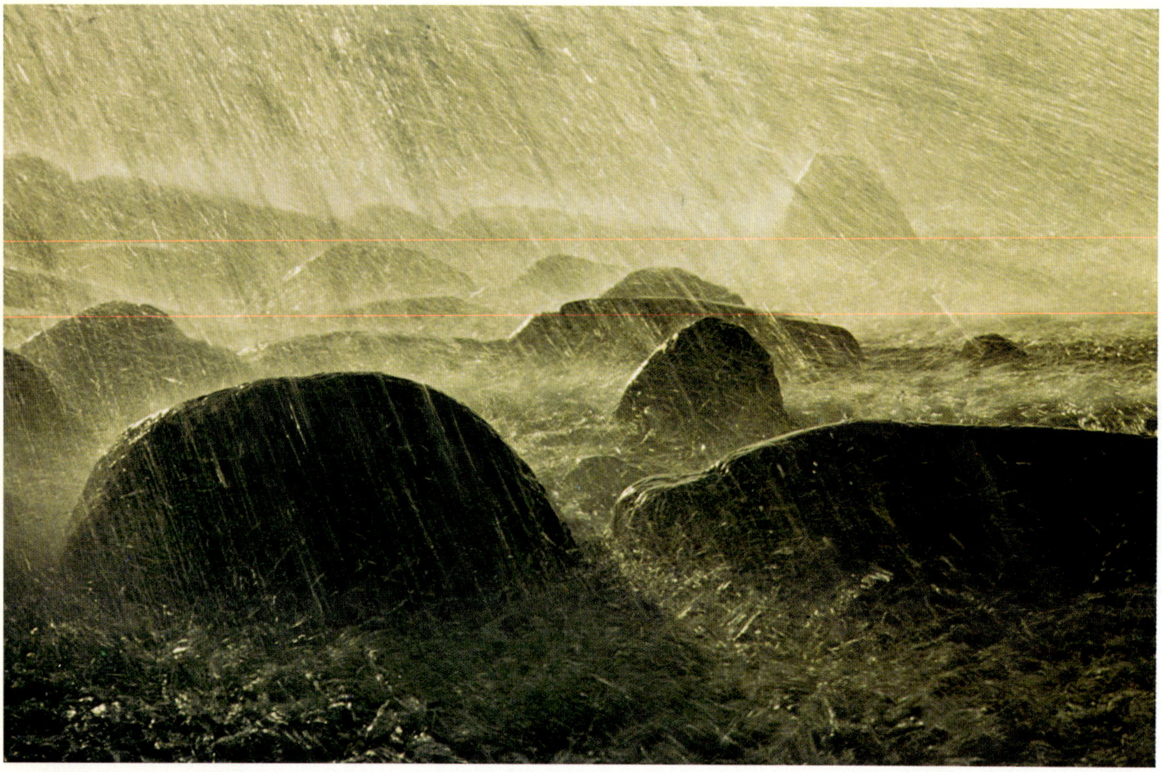
14

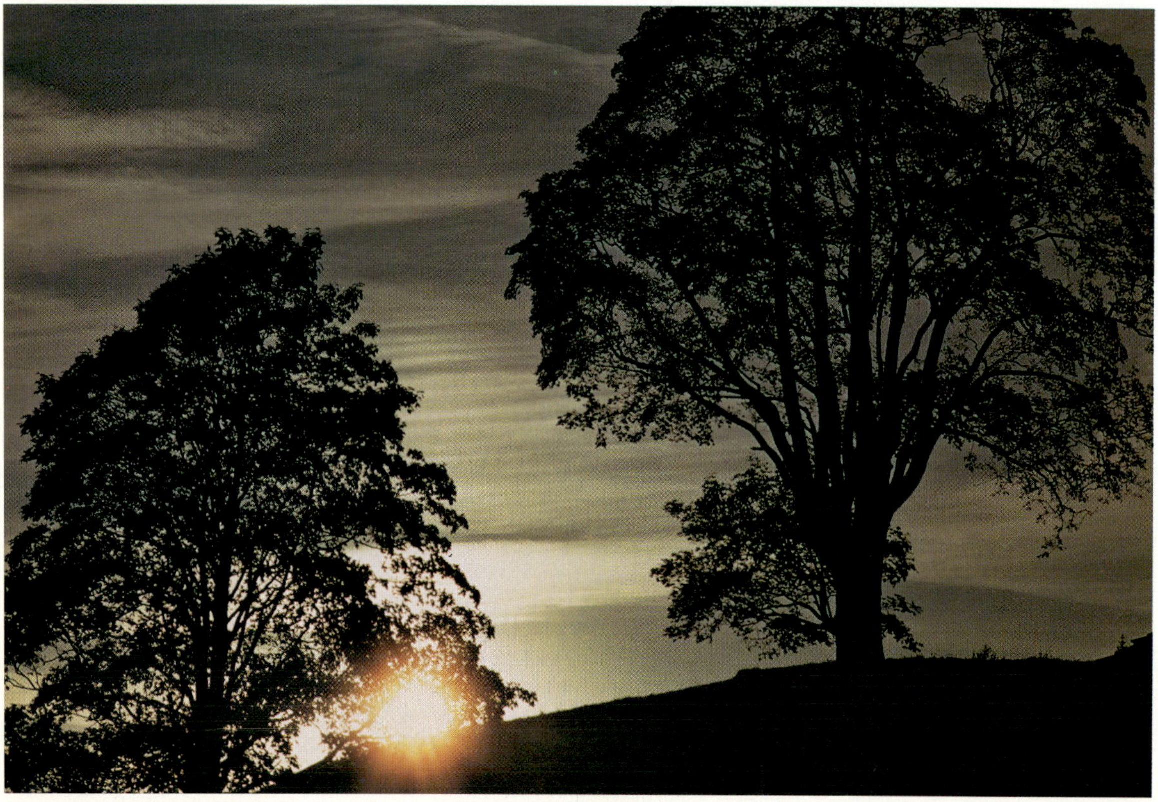
15

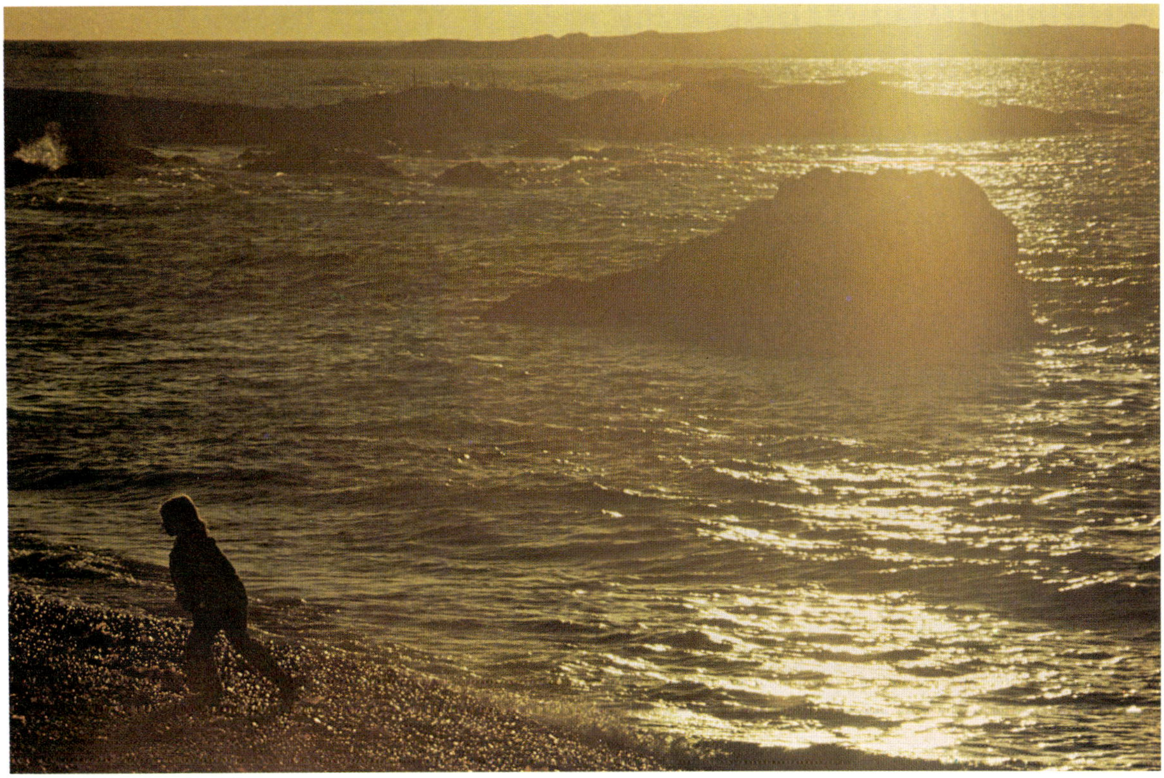

16

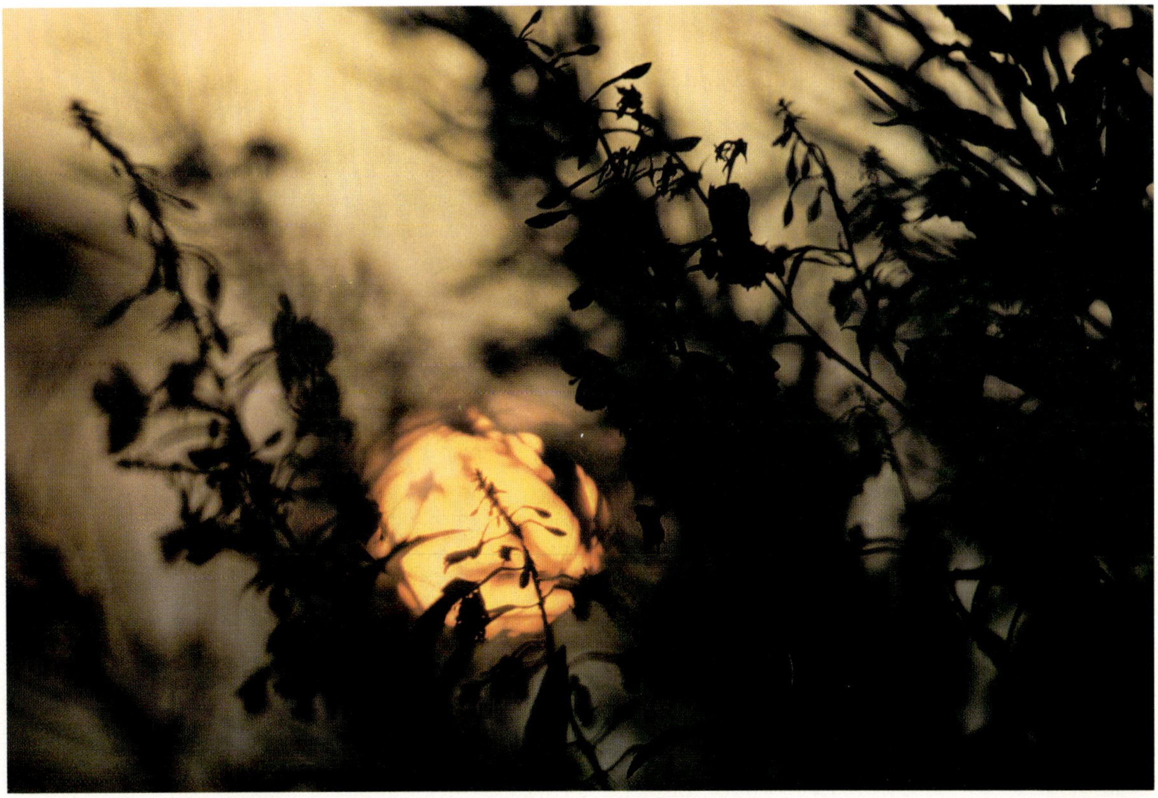

17

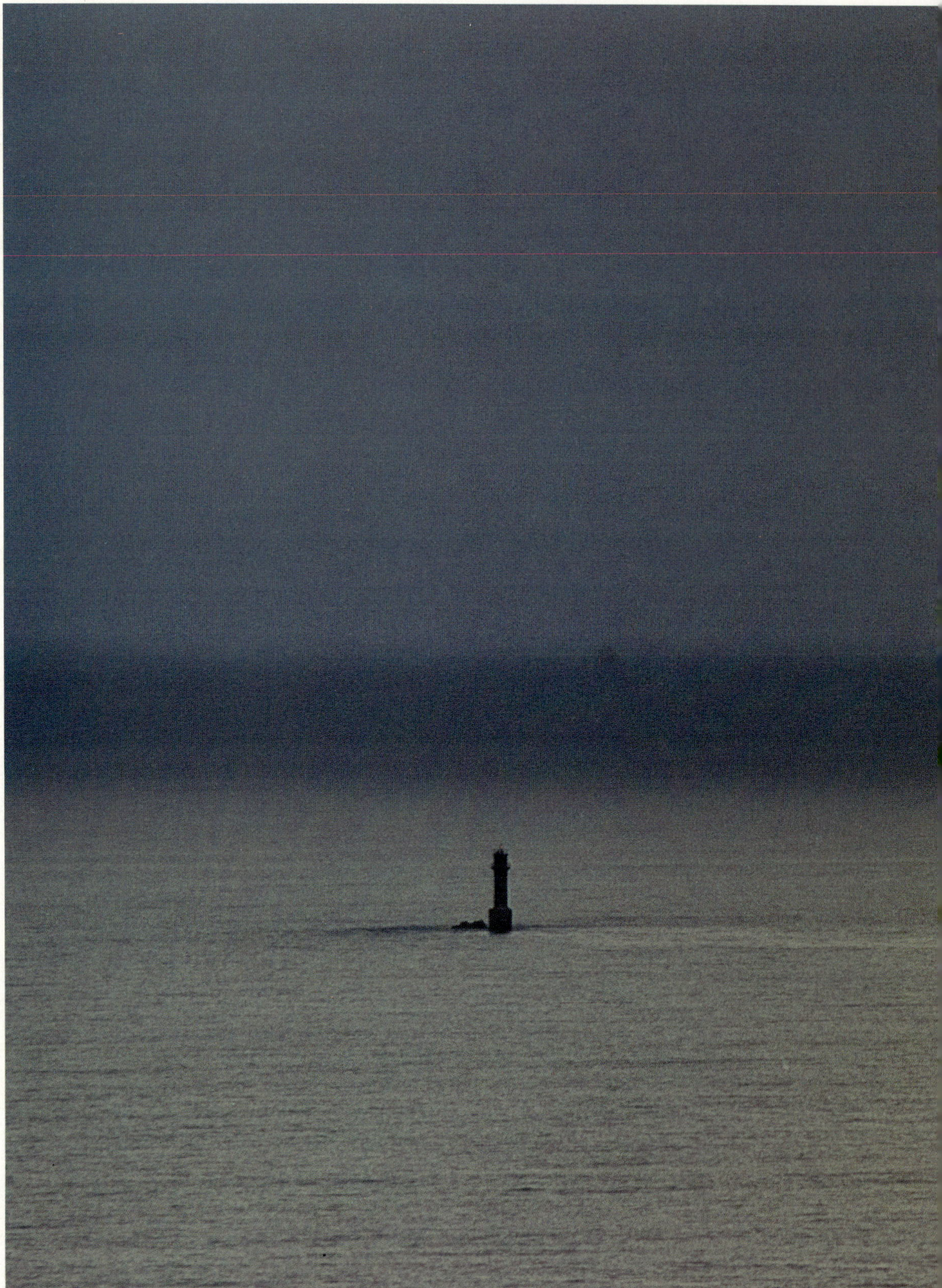

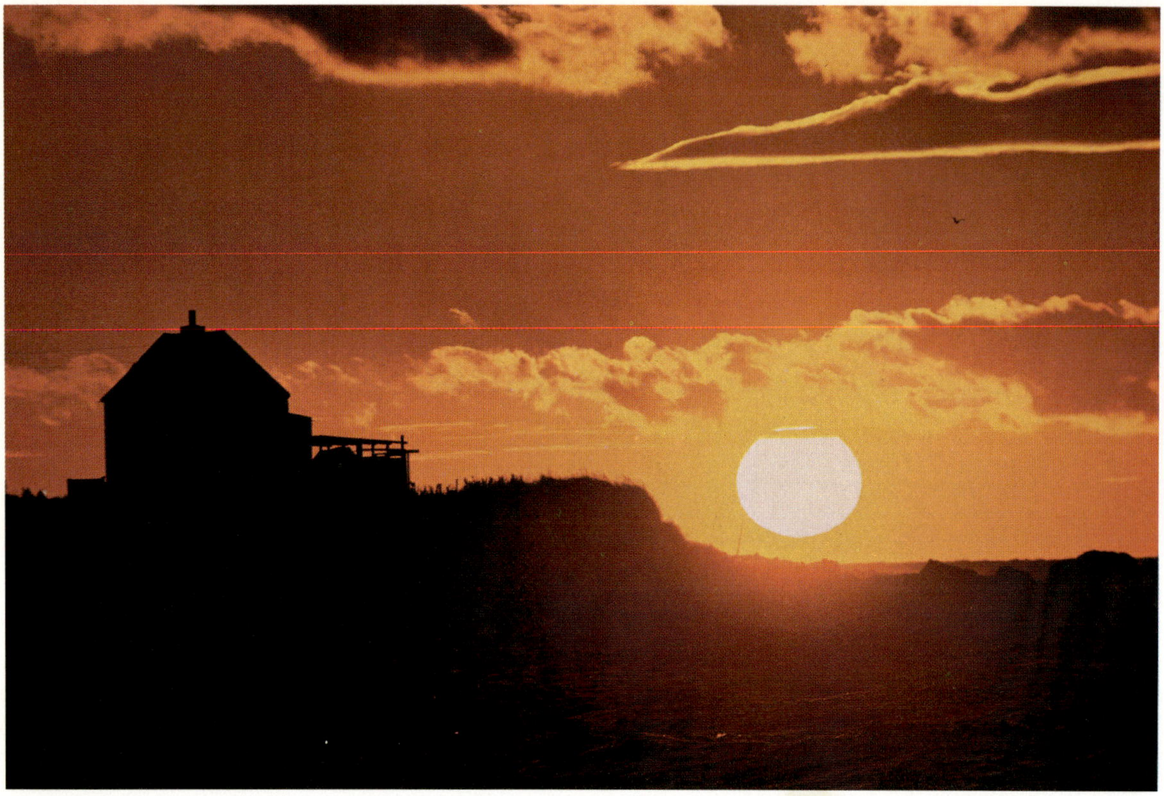
19

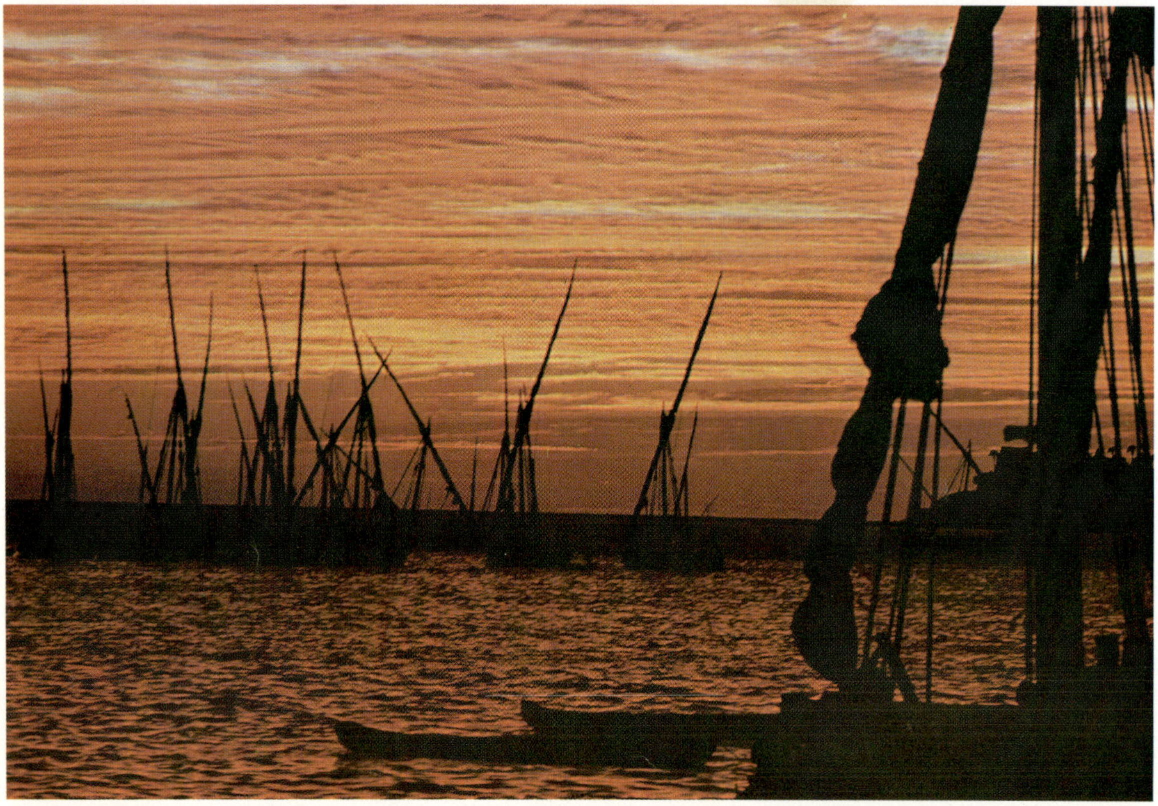
20

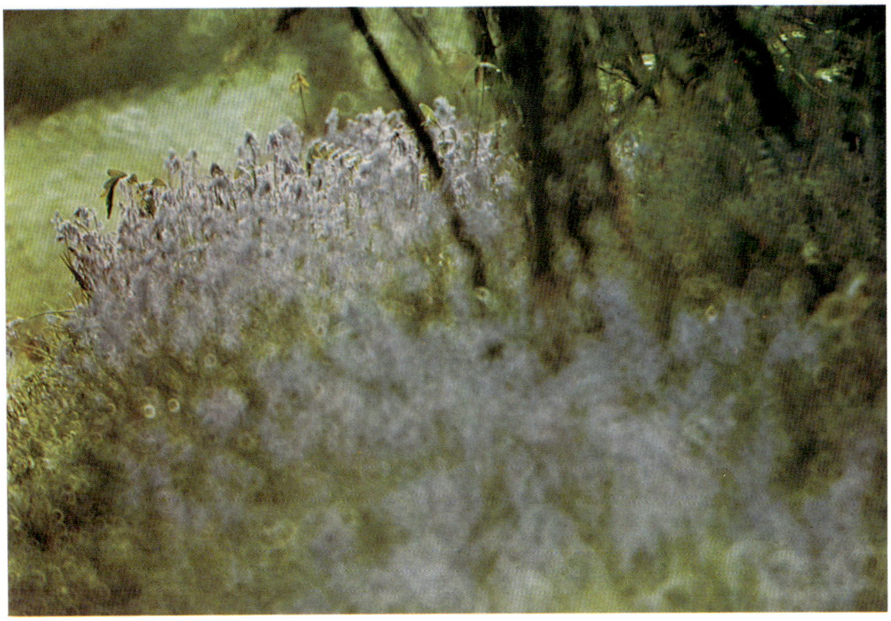

21

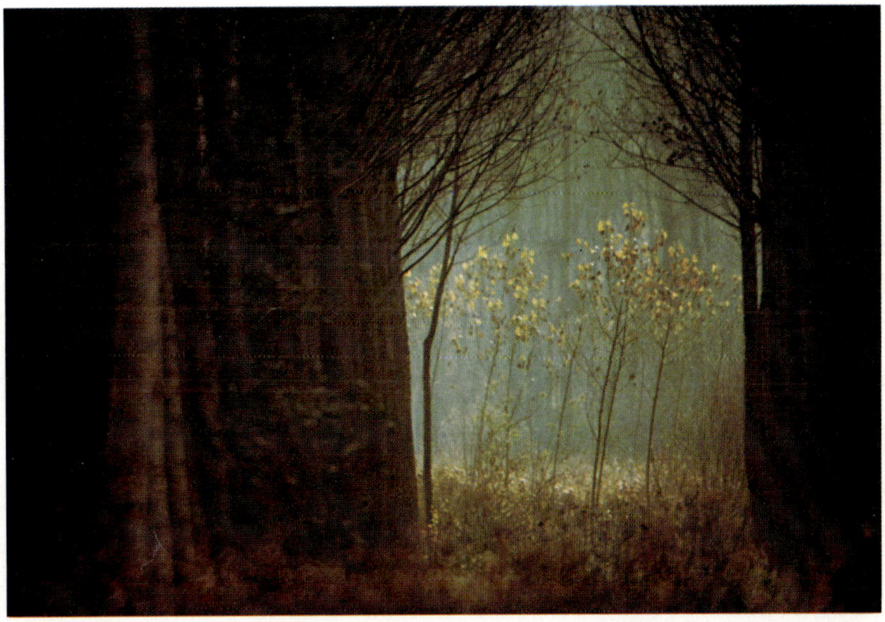

22

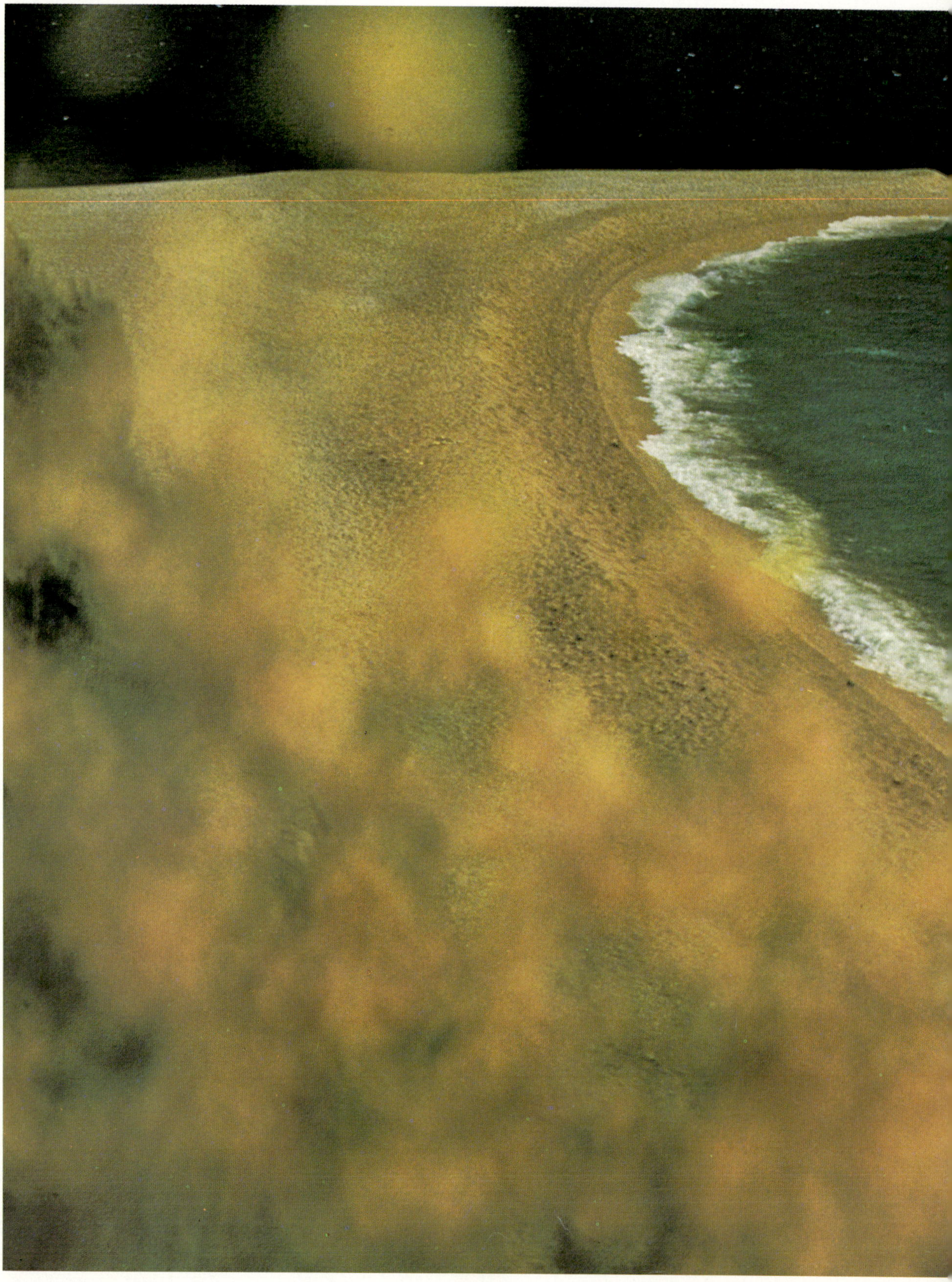

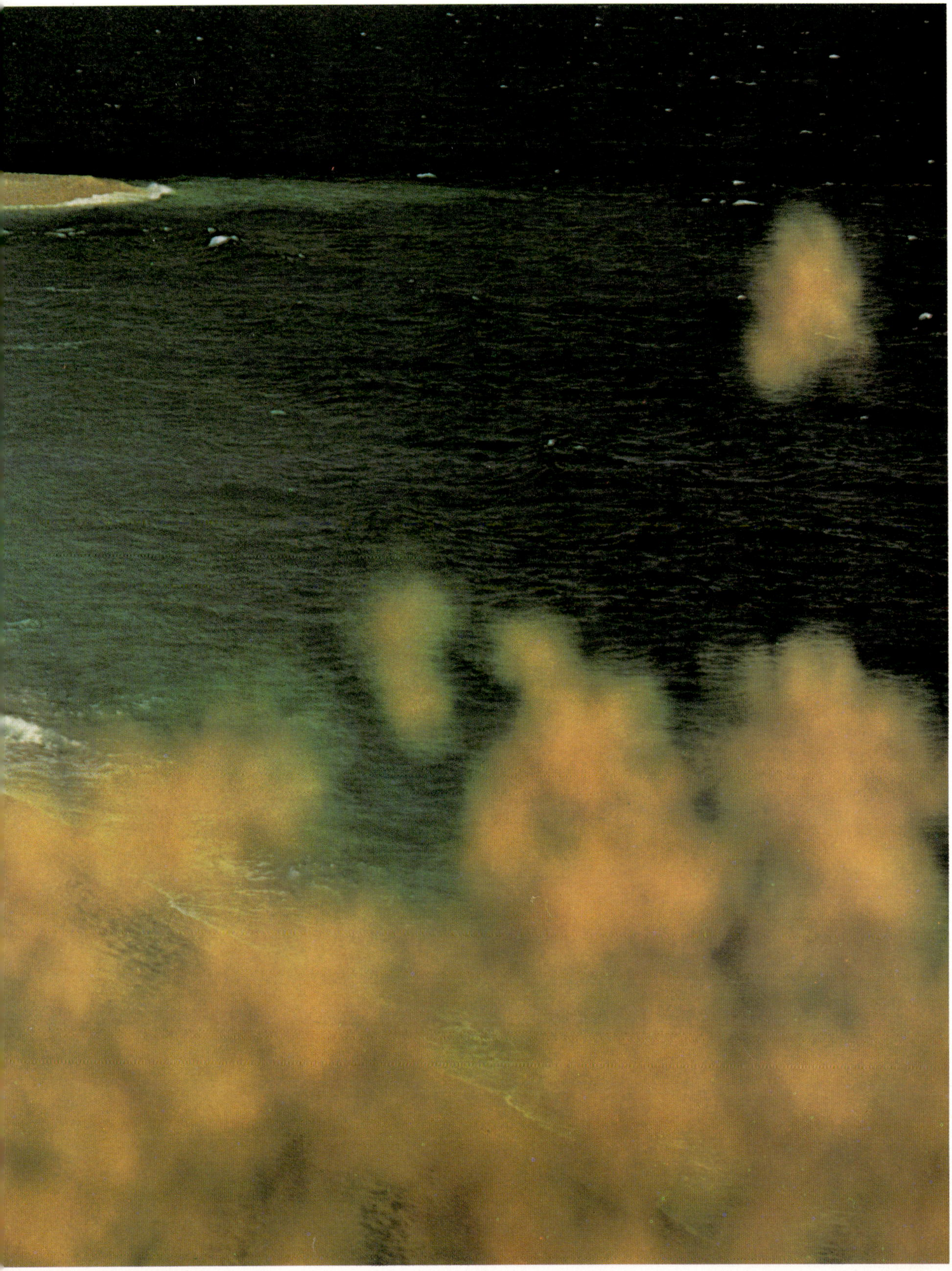

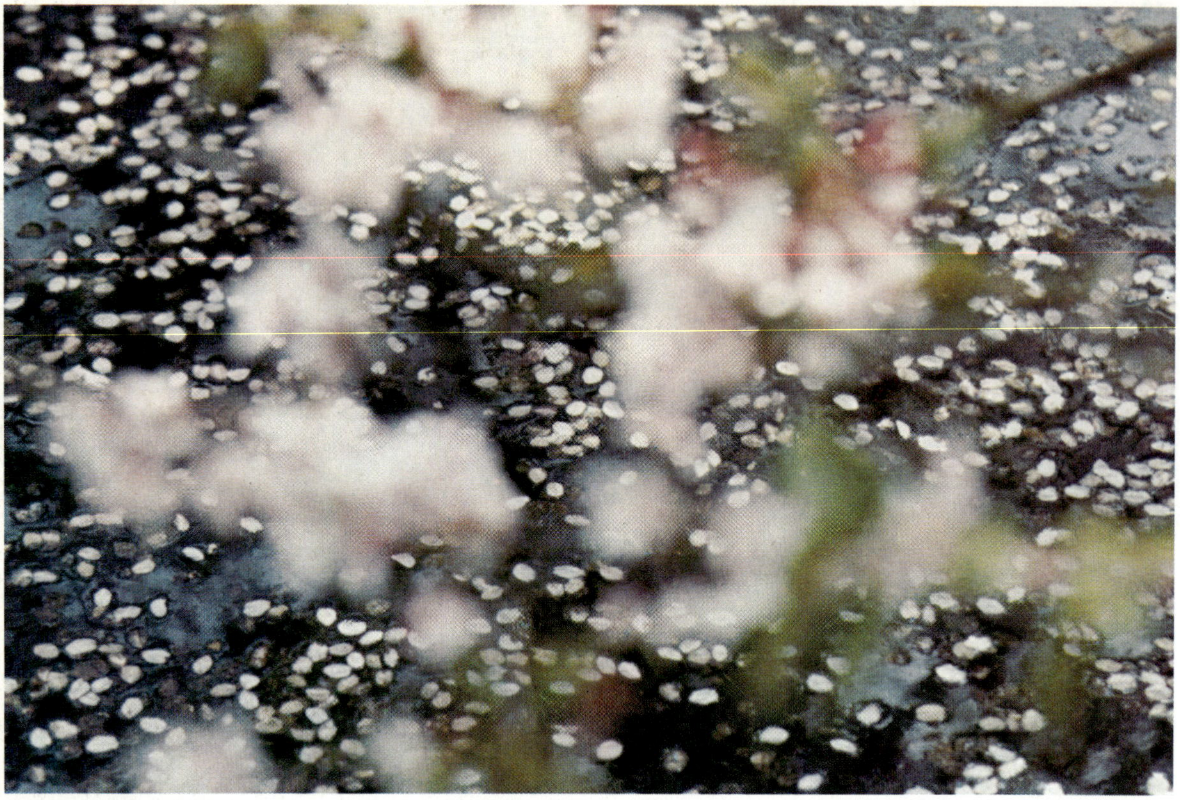

24

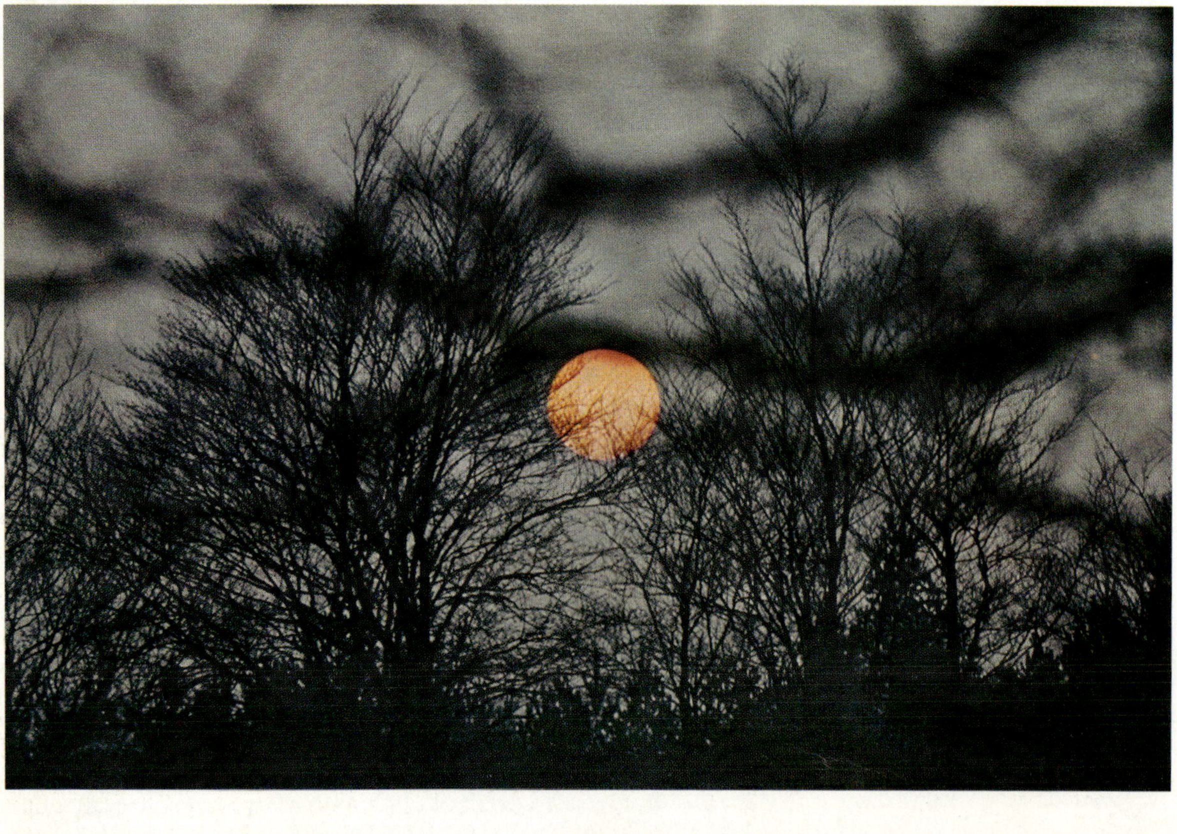

25

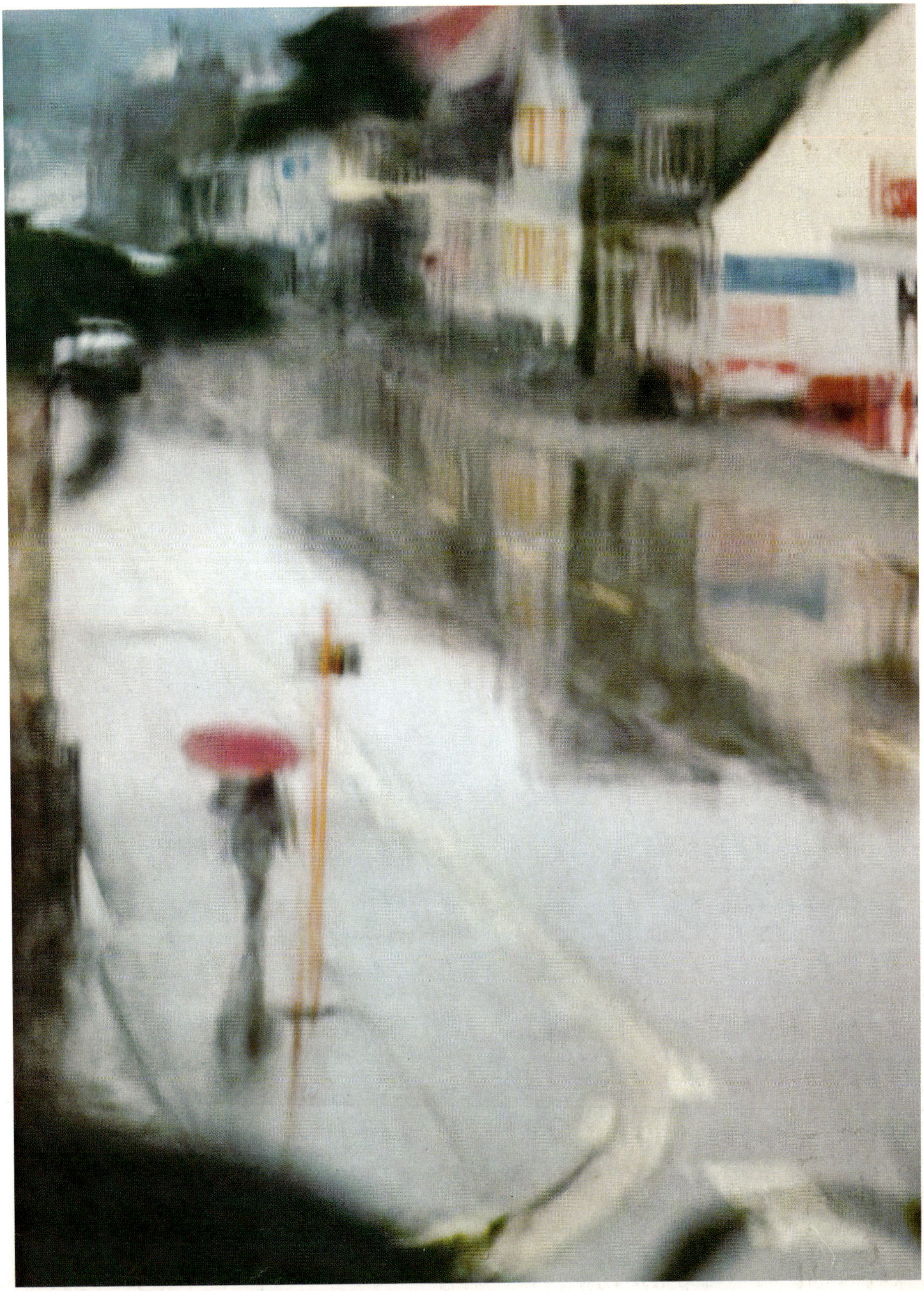

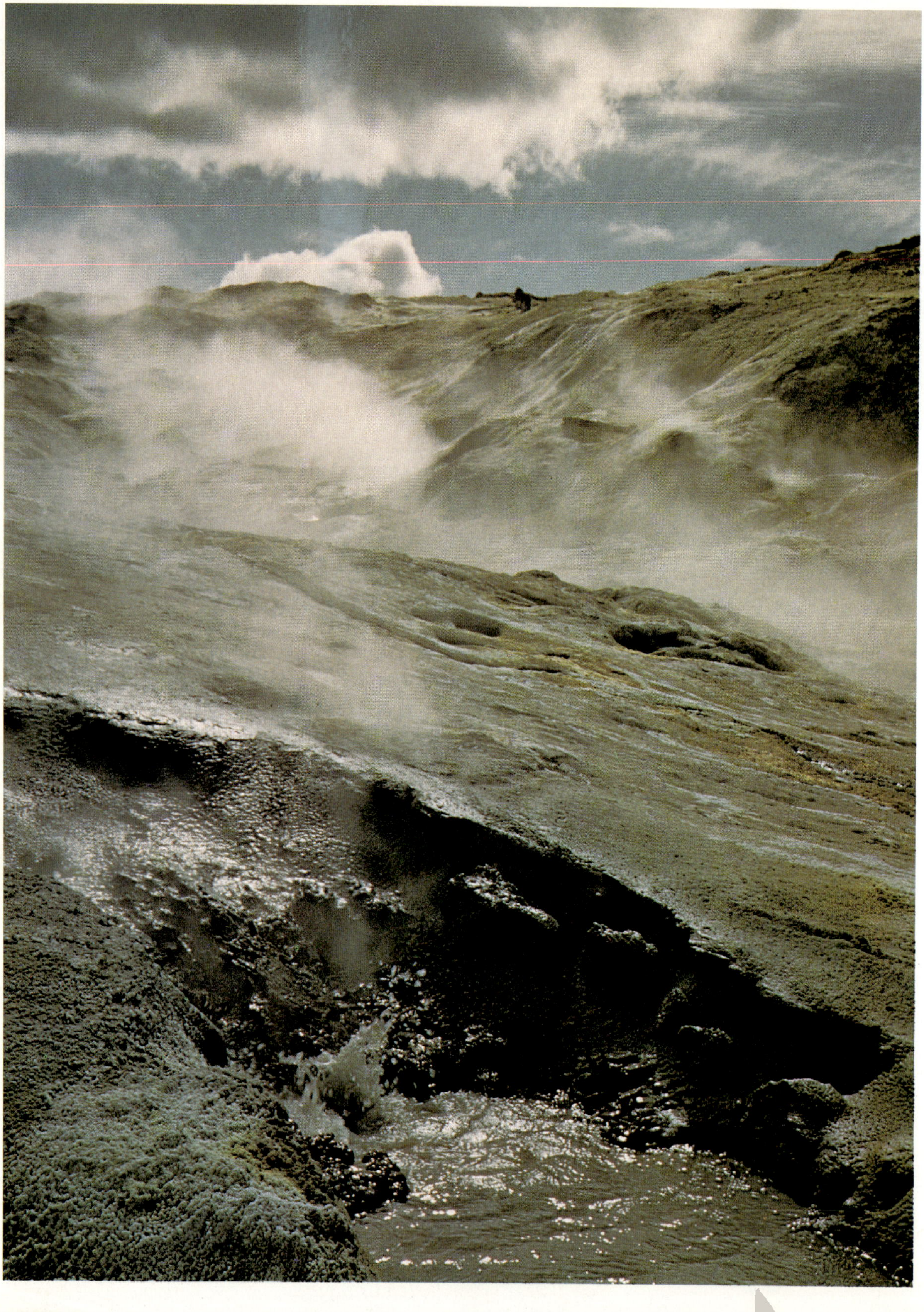

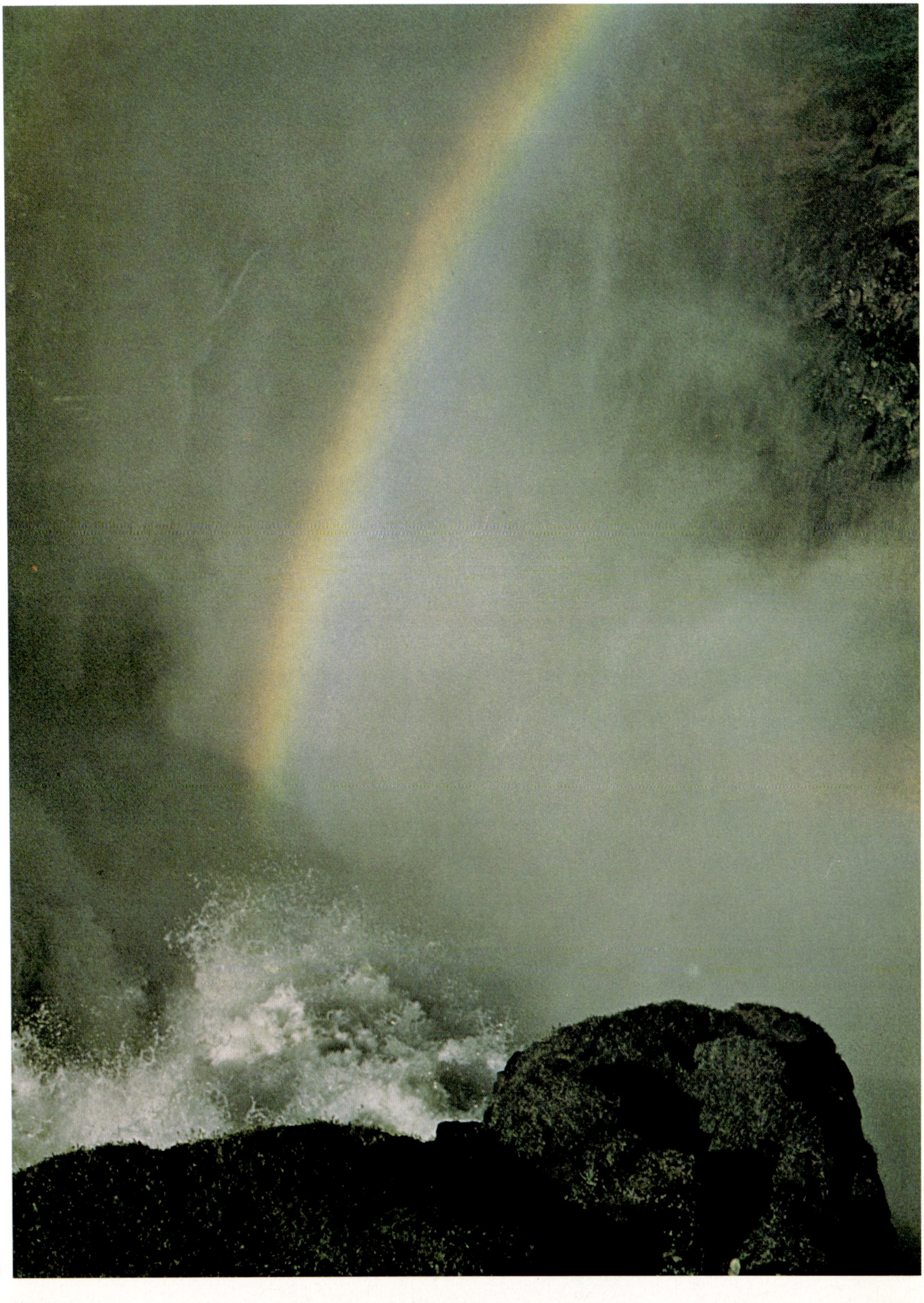

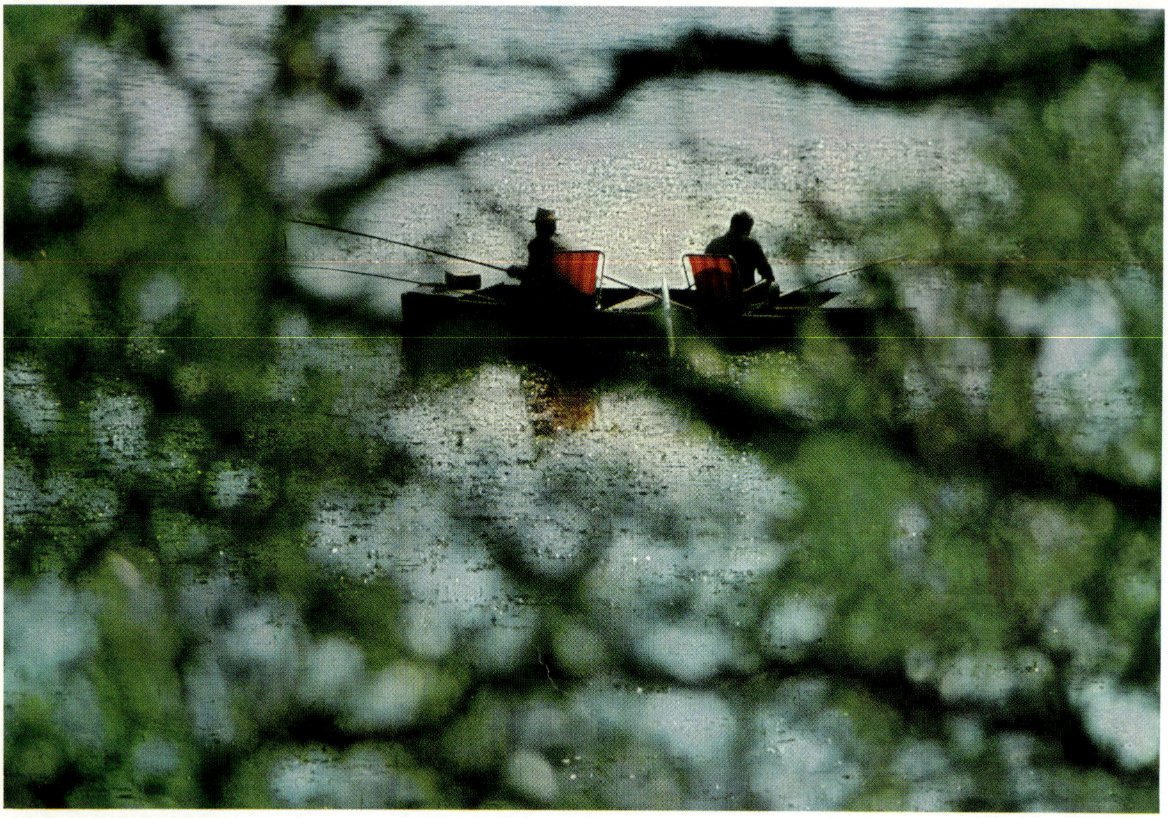

29

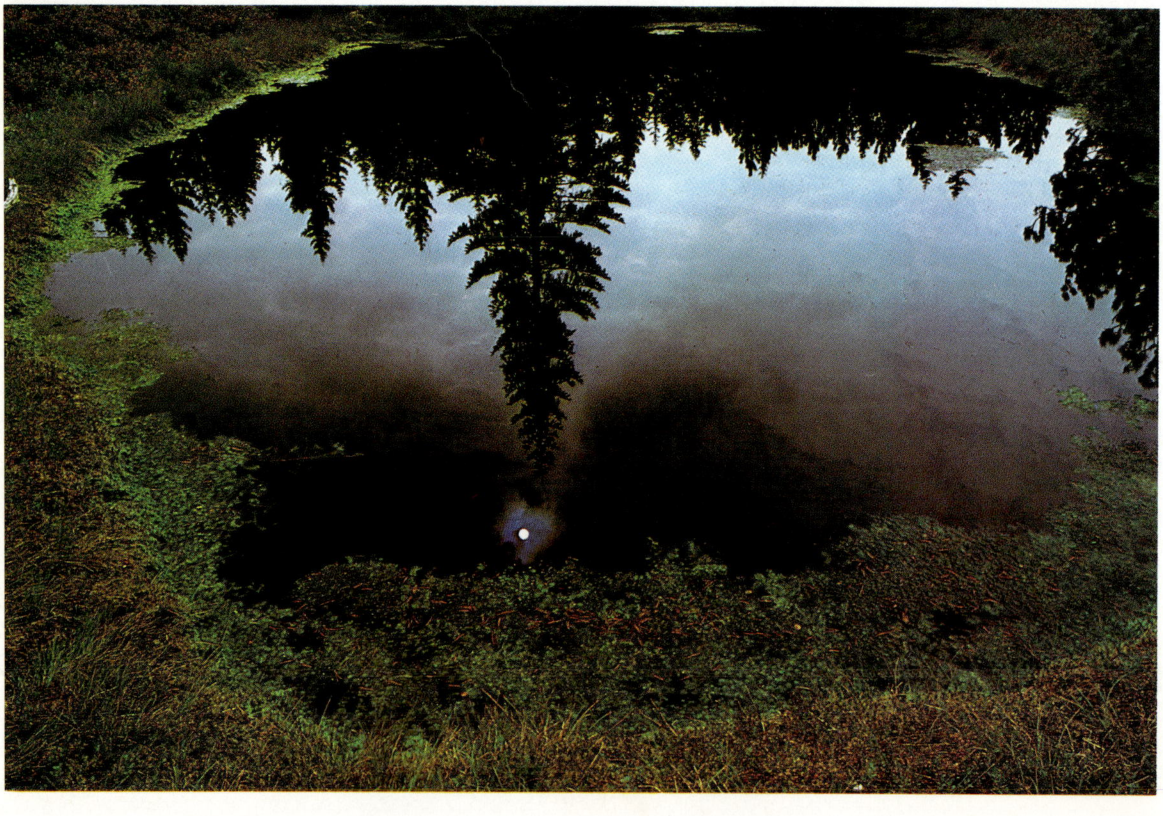

30

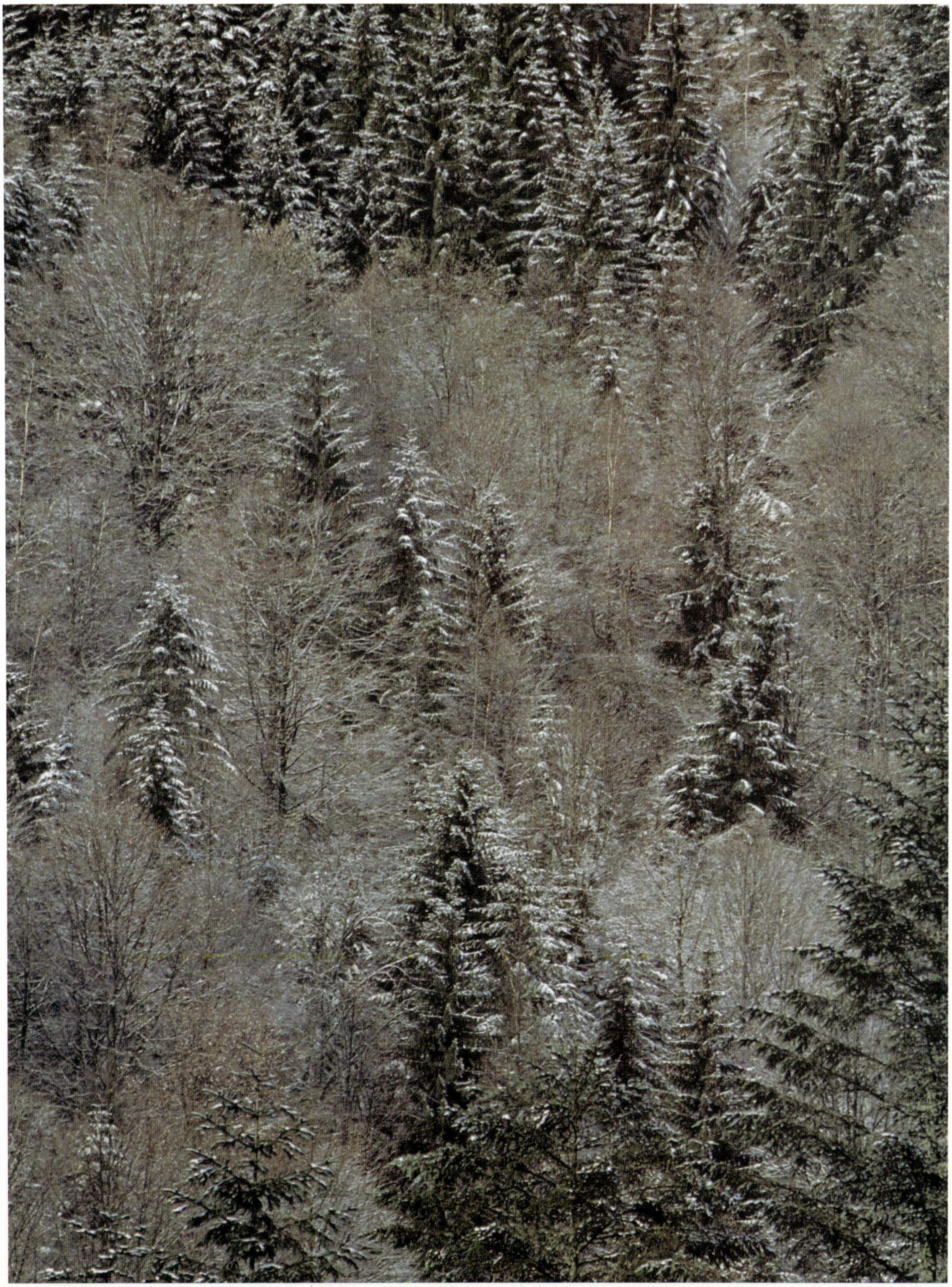

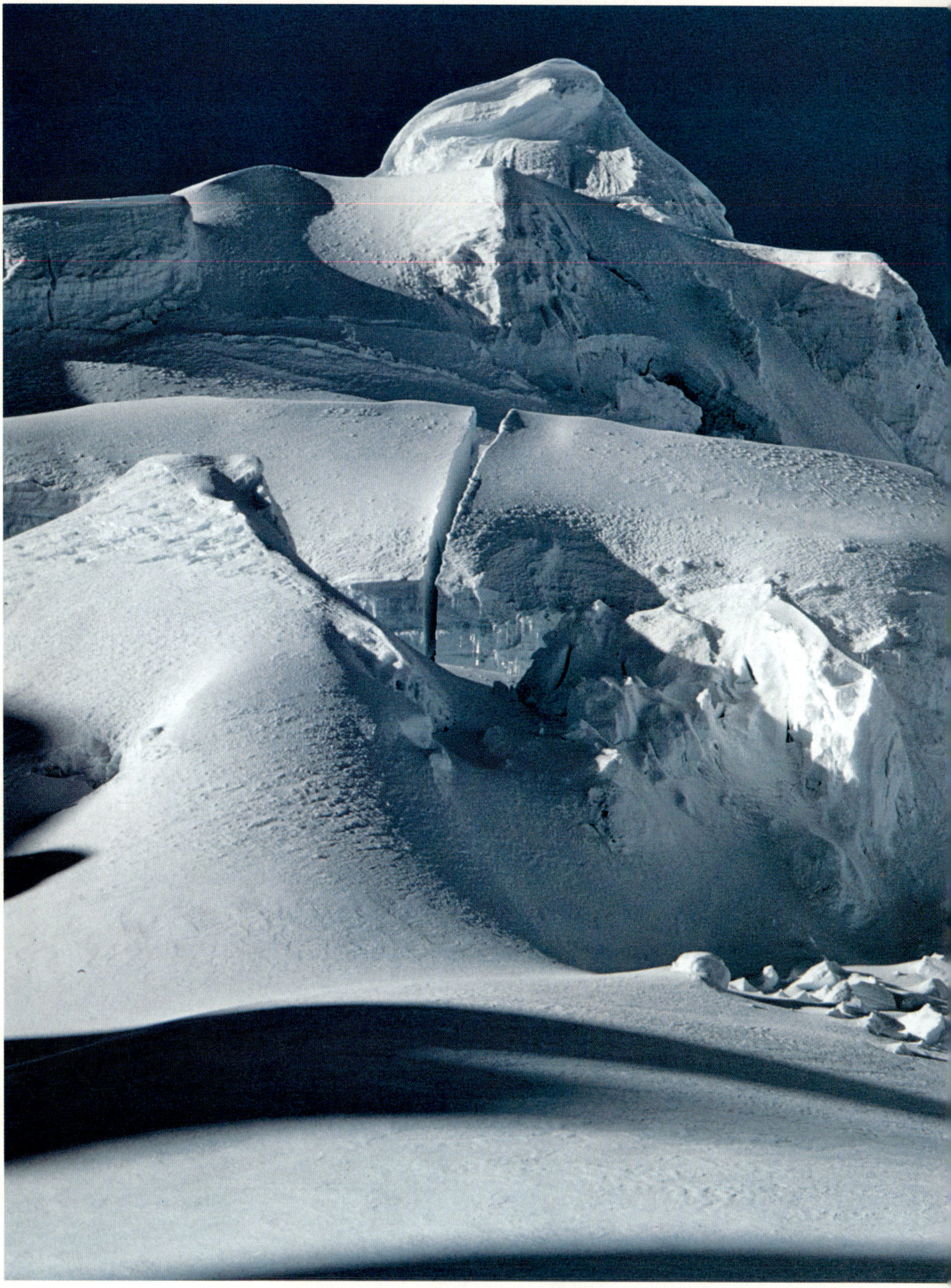

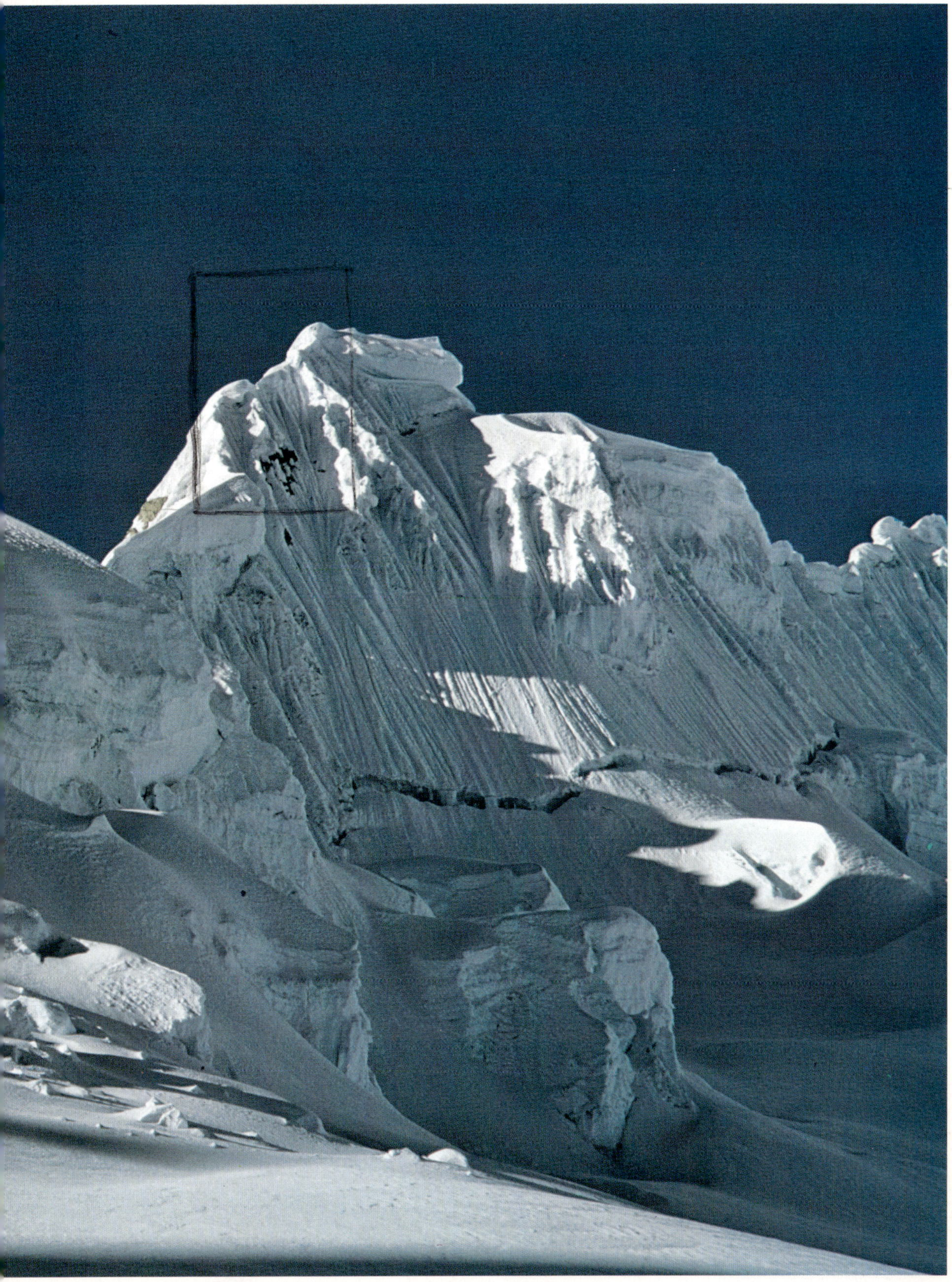

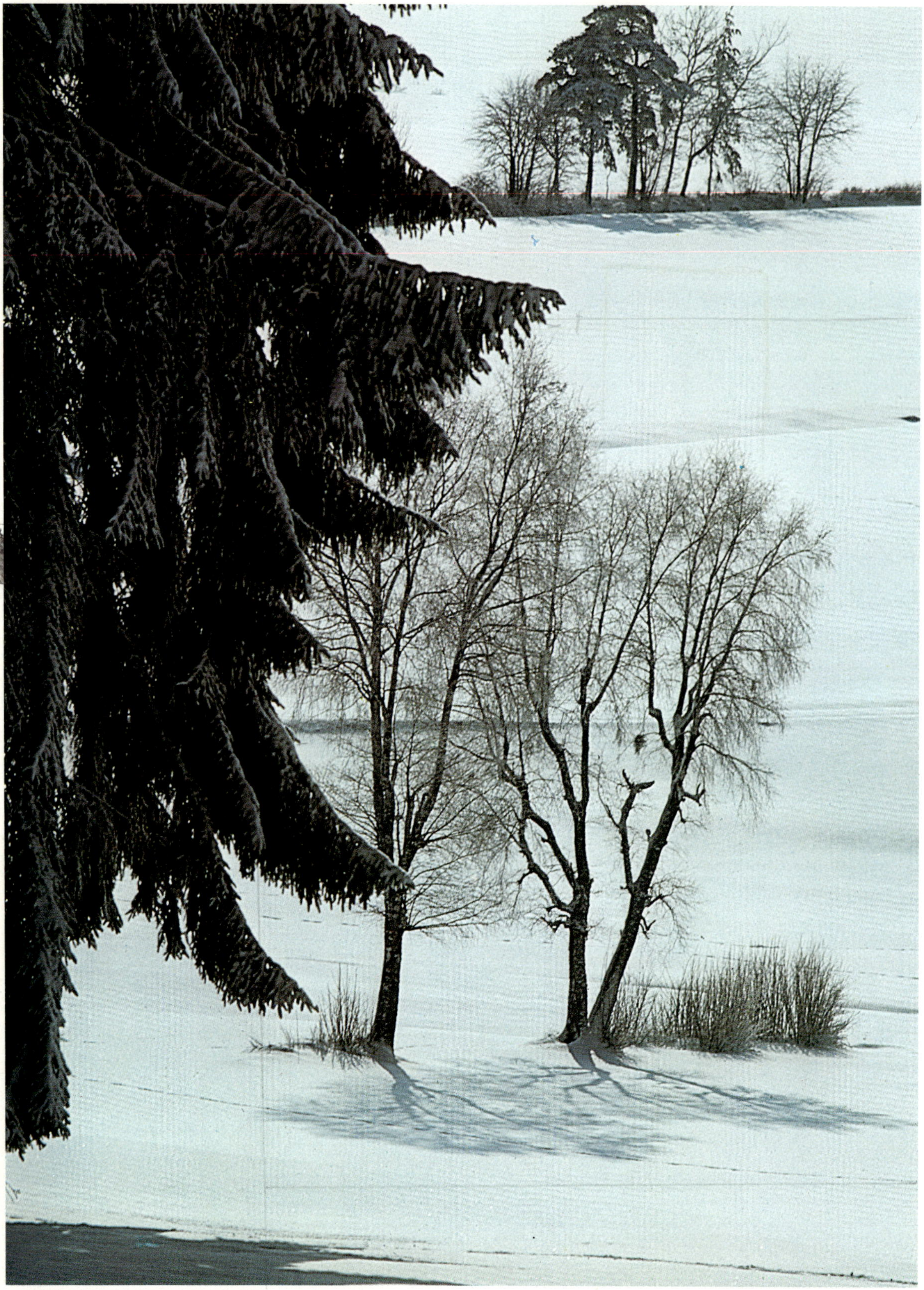

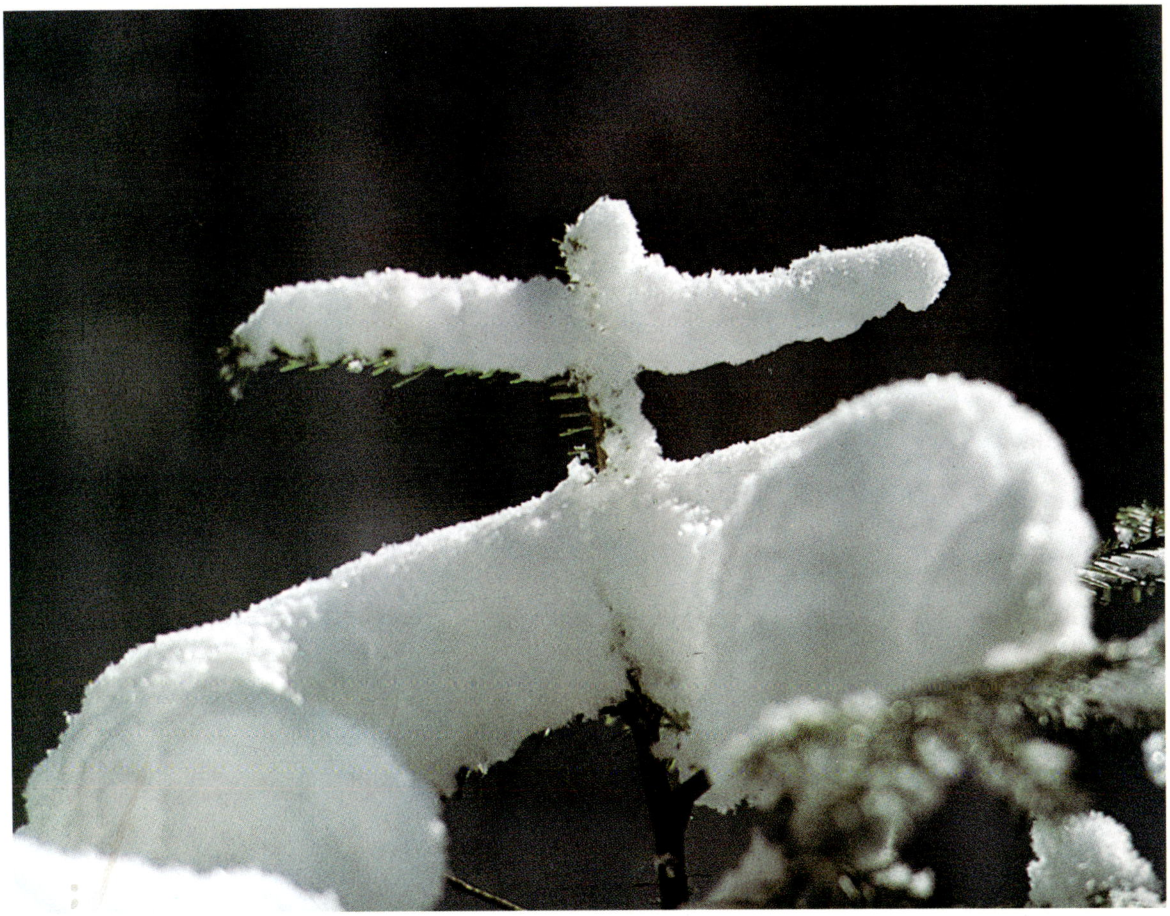

34

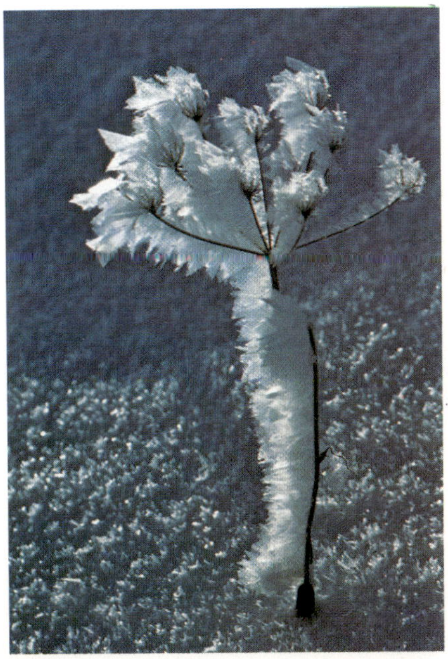

35

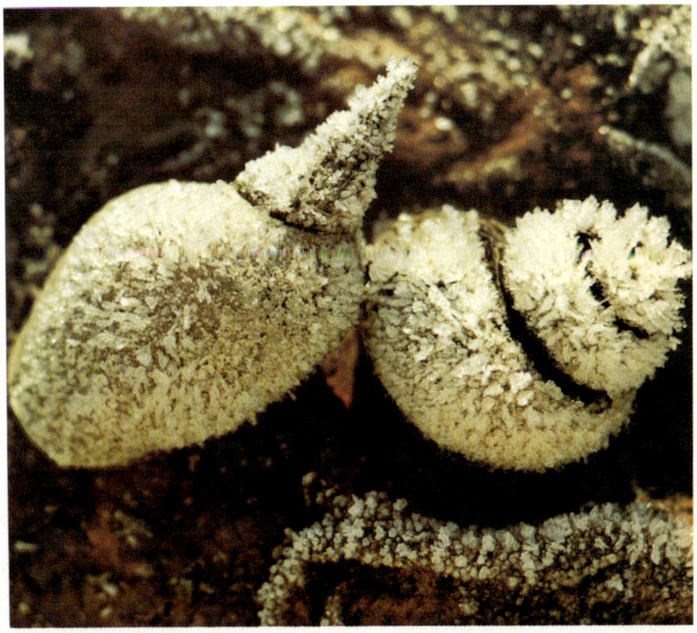

36

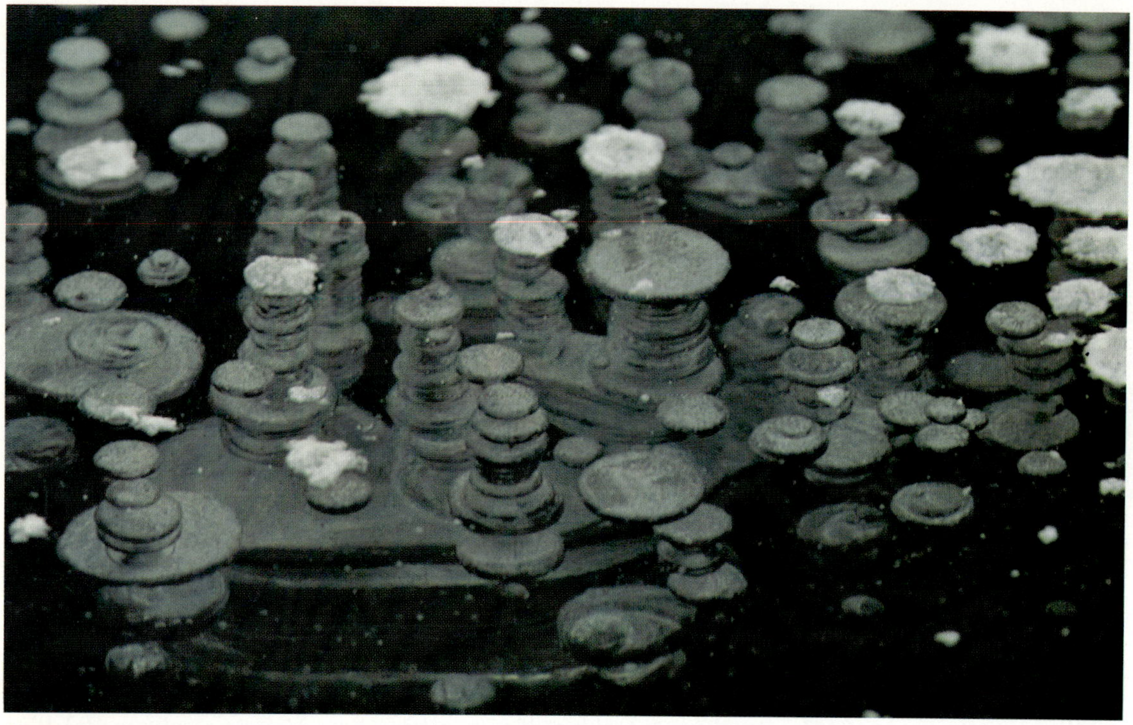

37

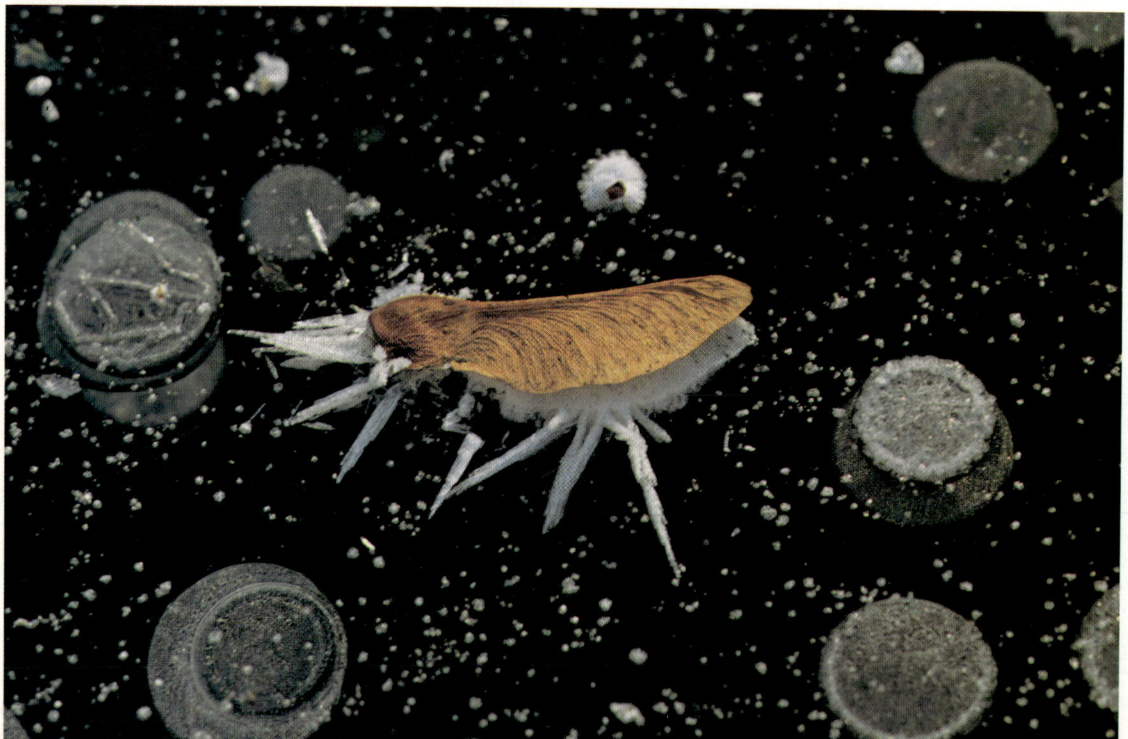

38

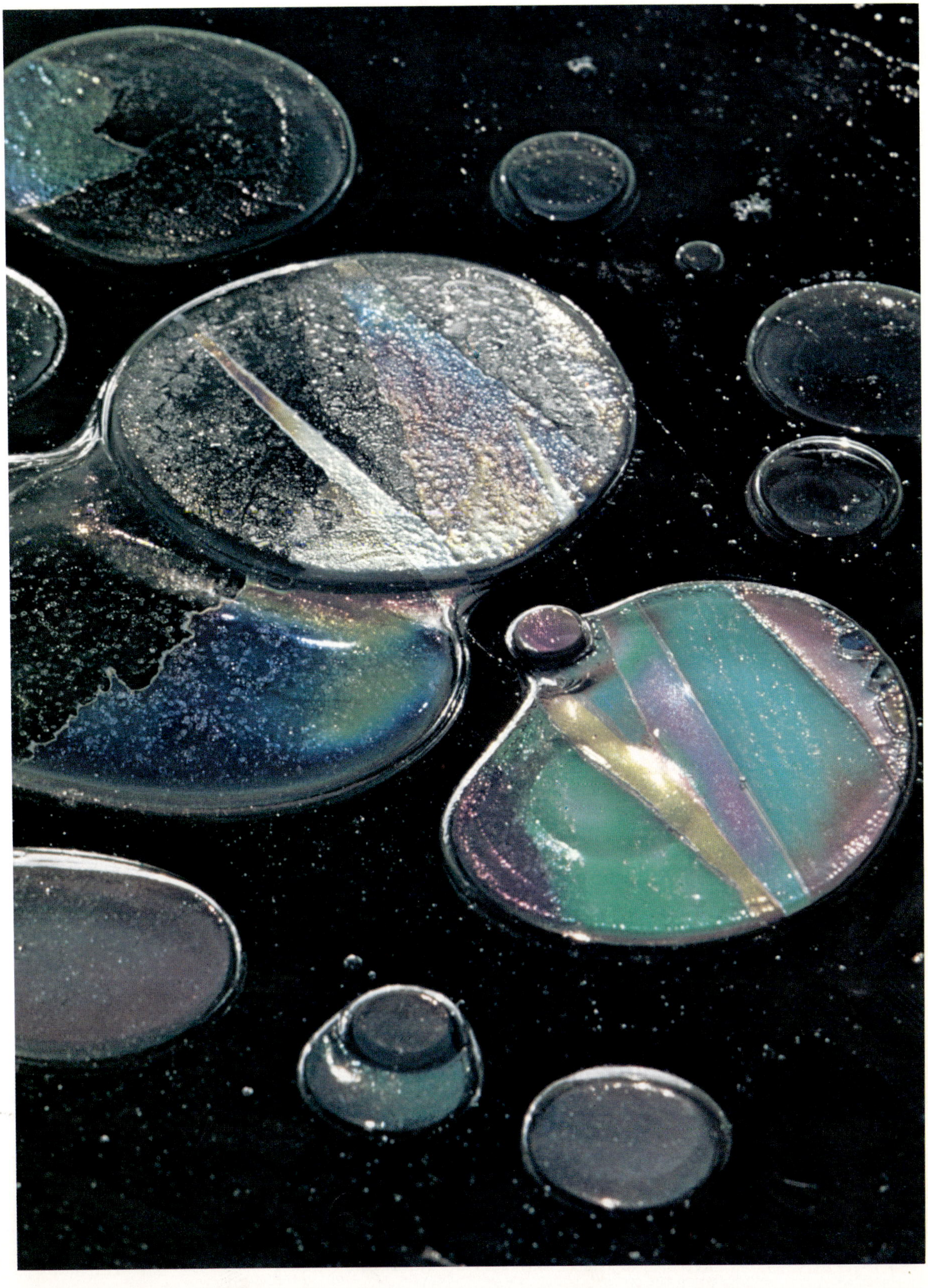

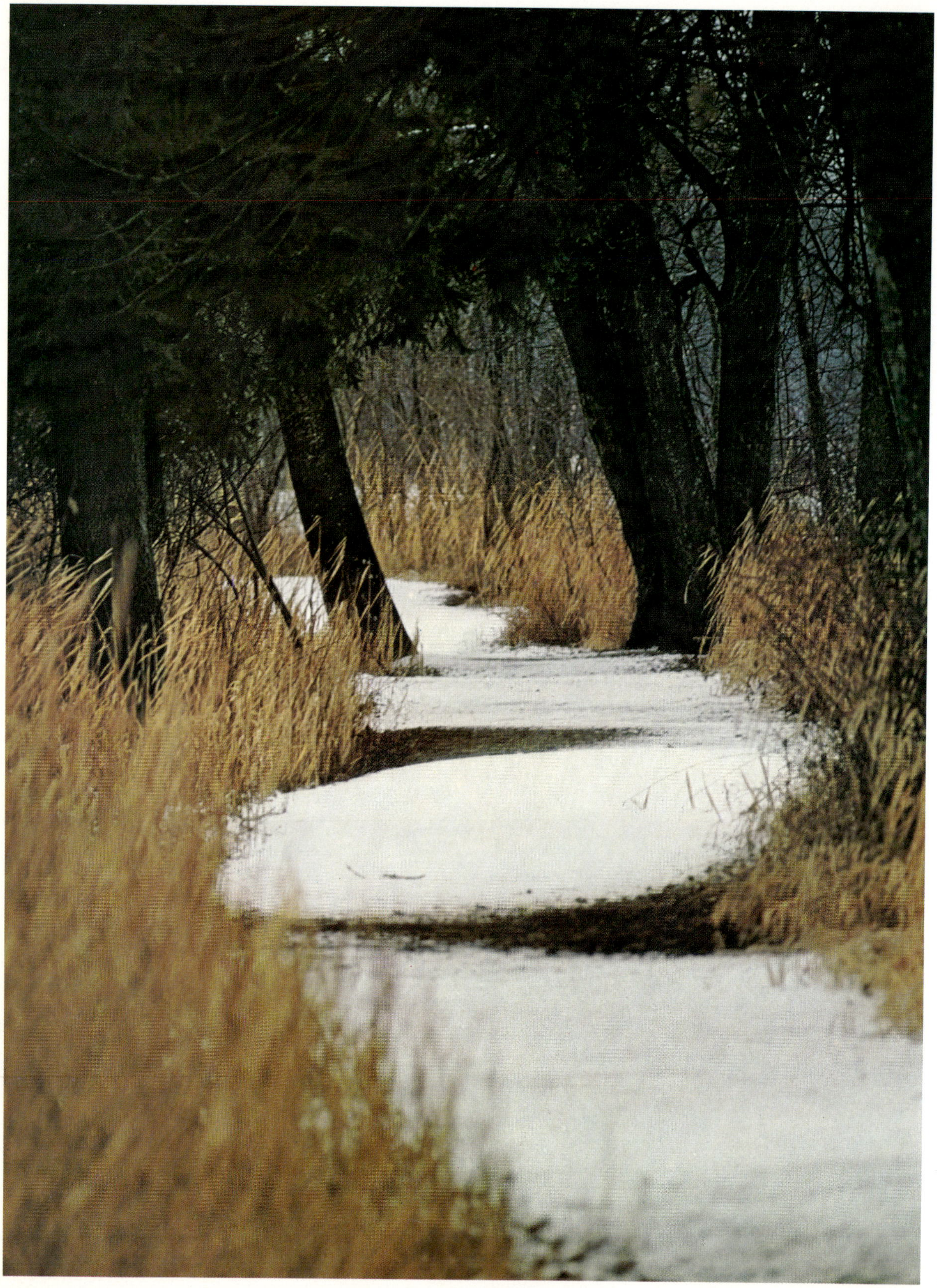

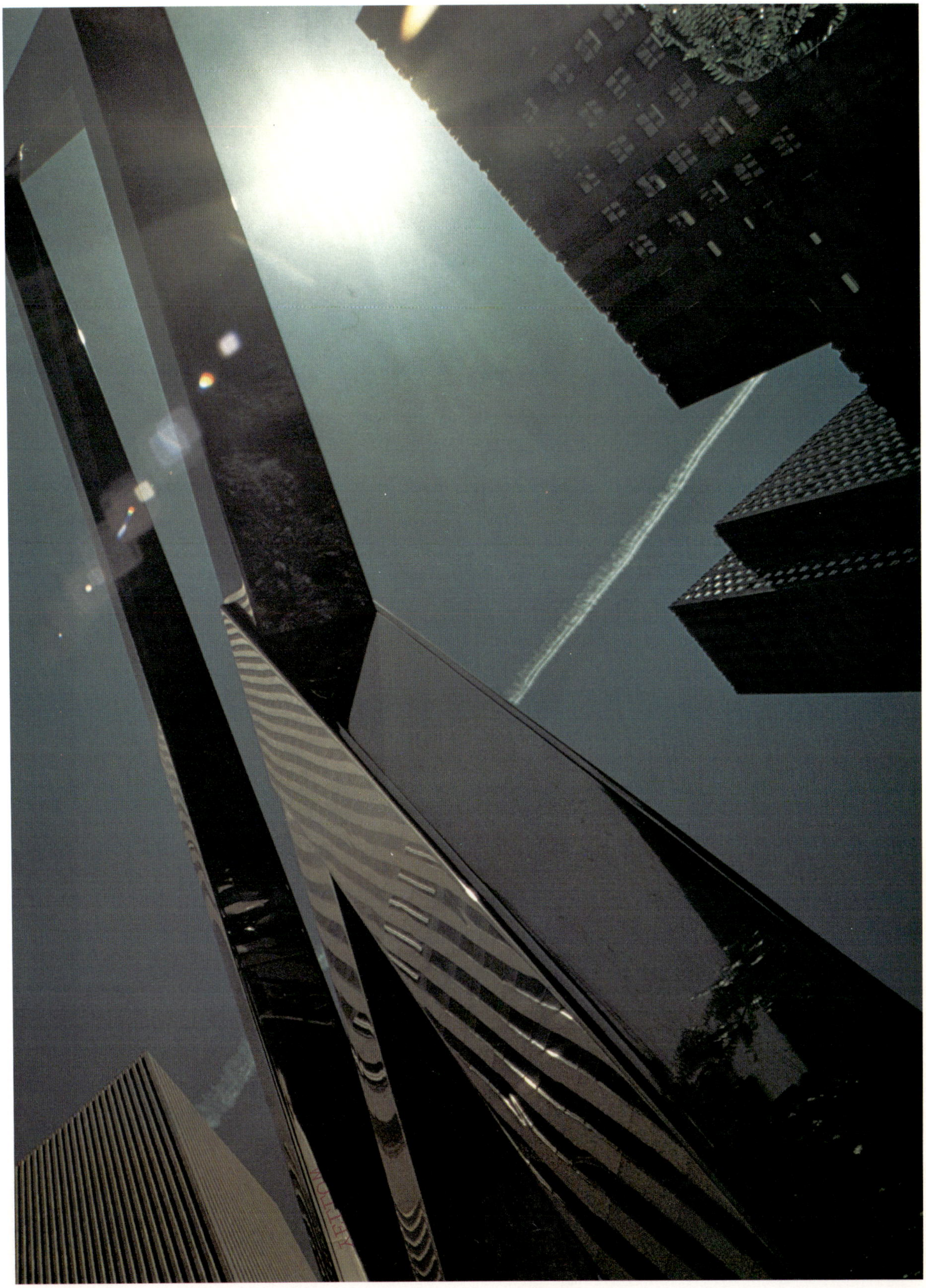

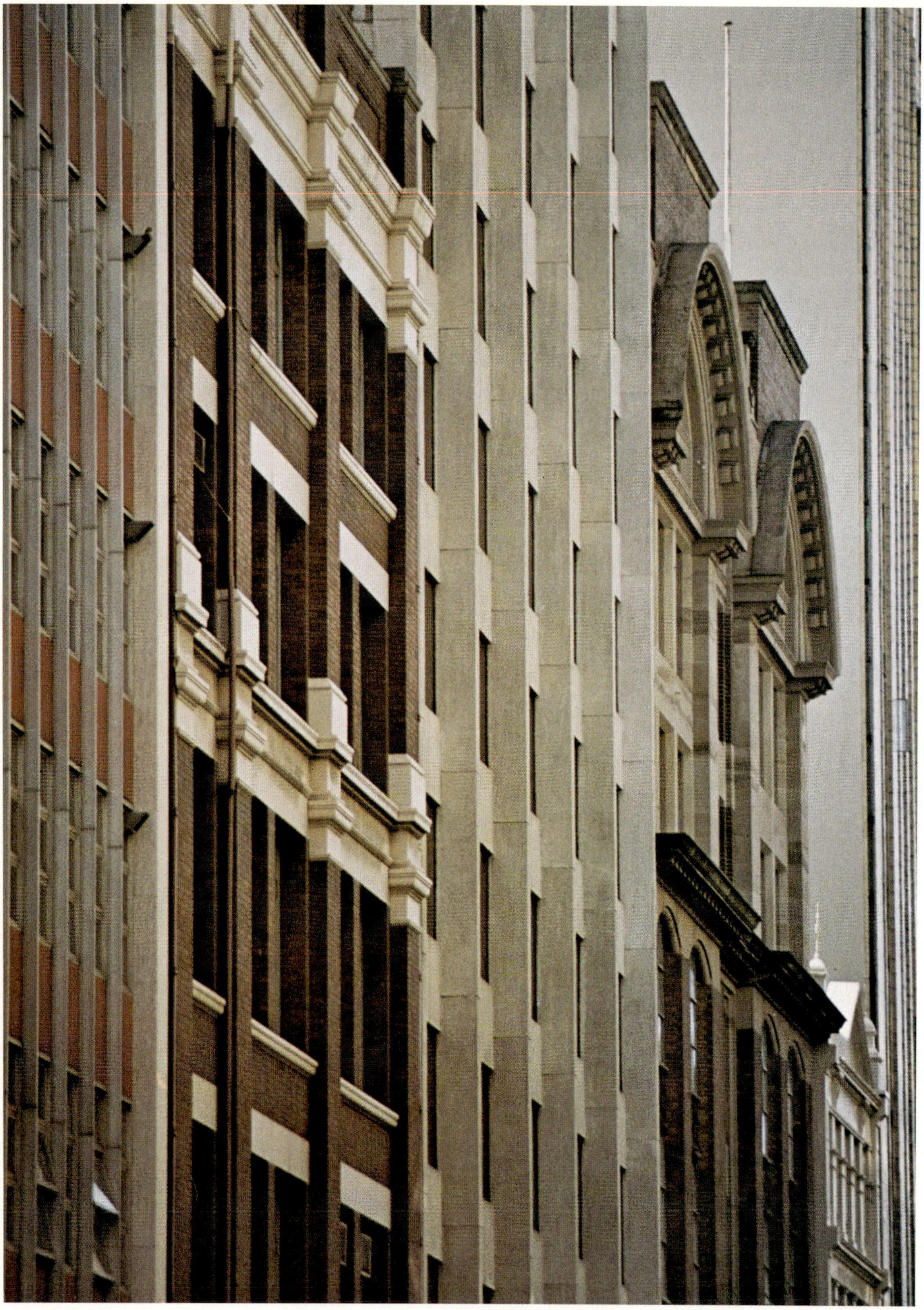

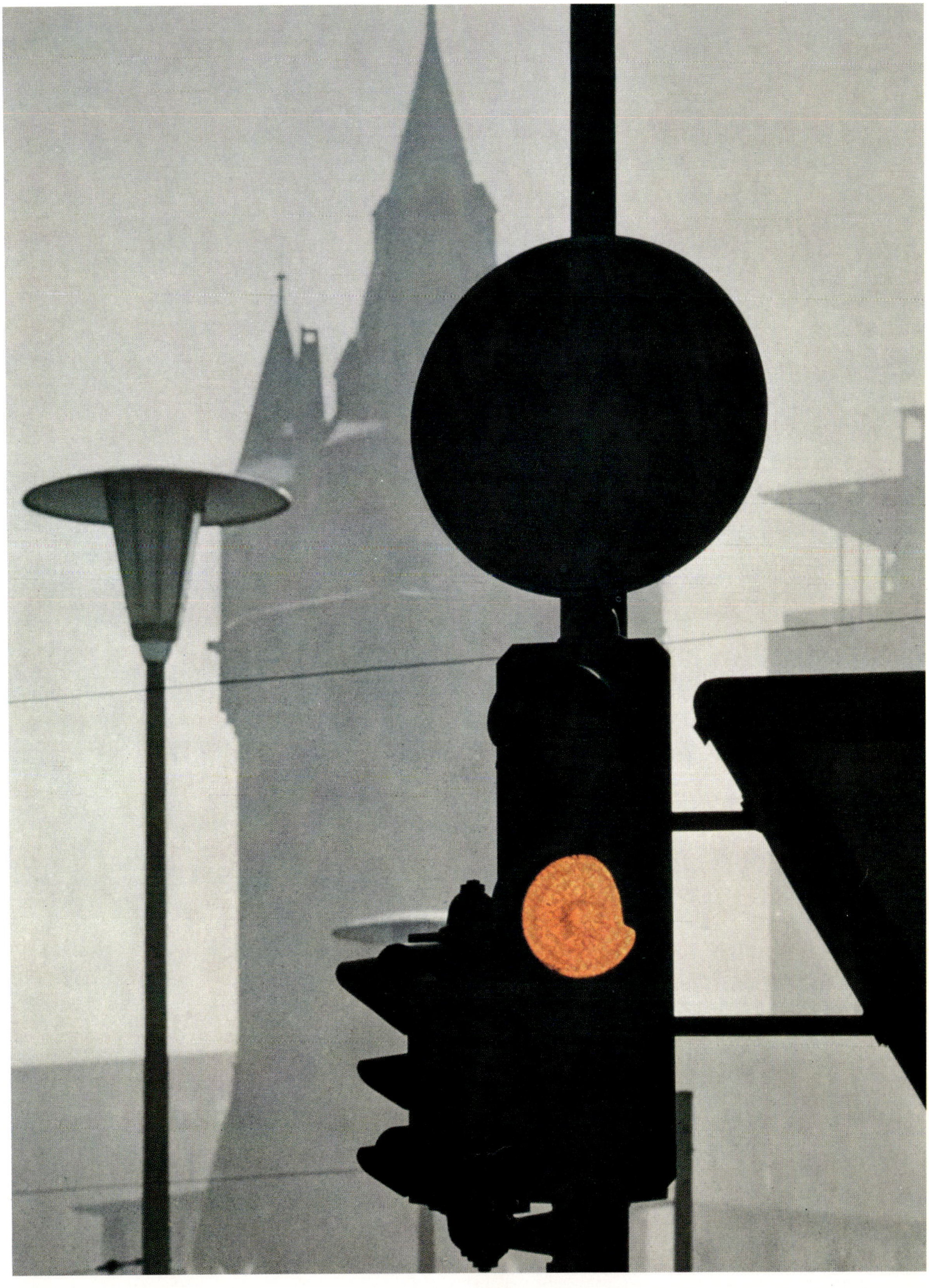

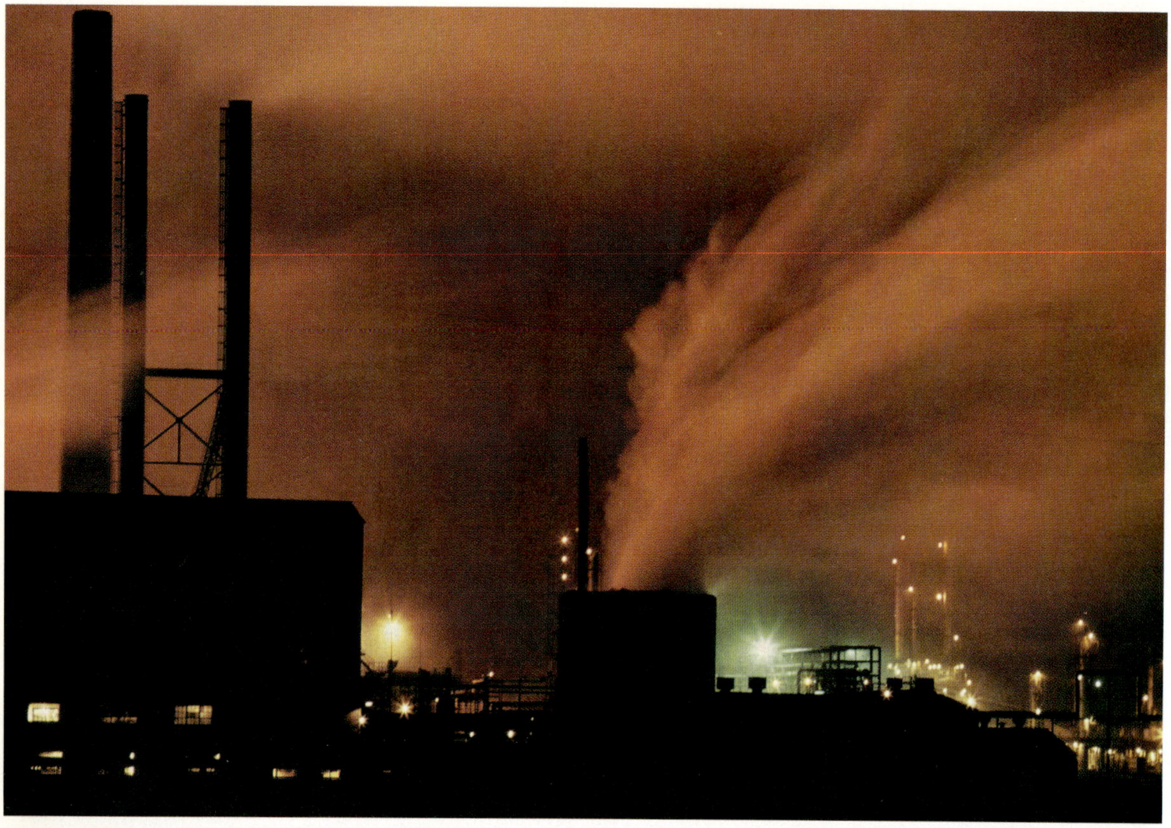
44

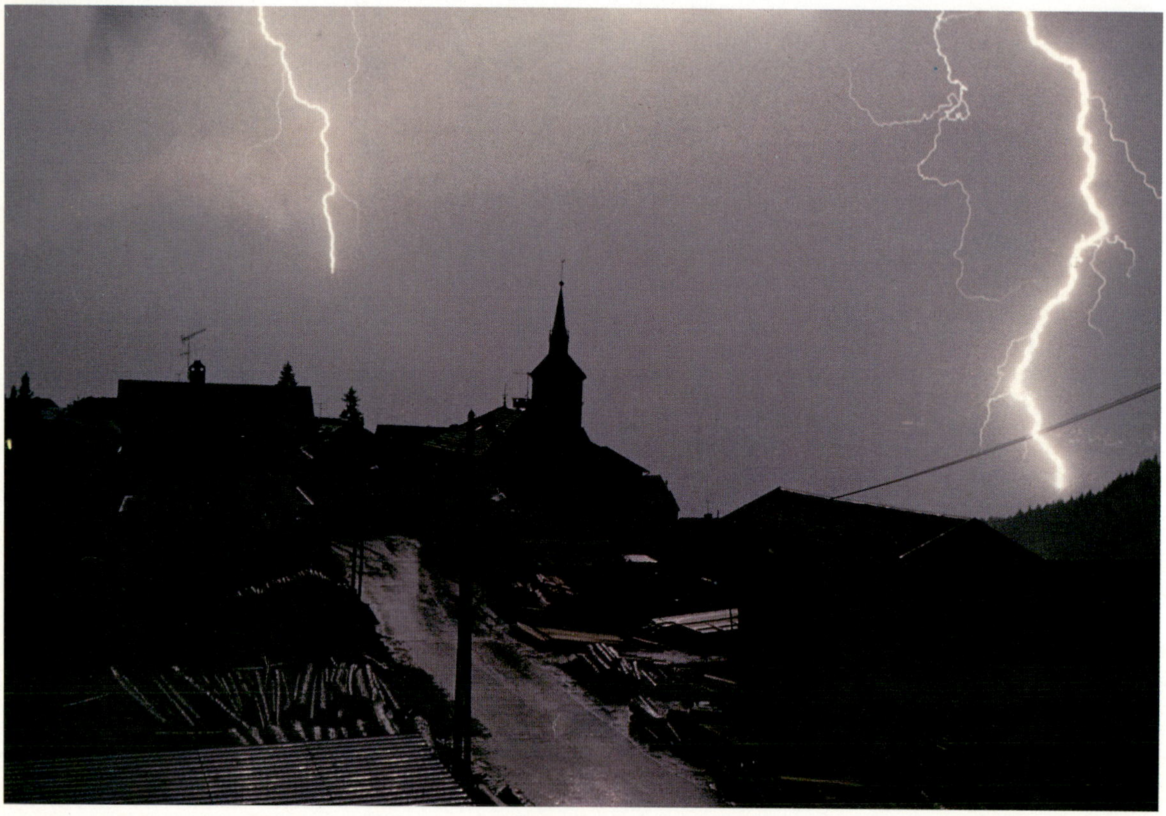
45

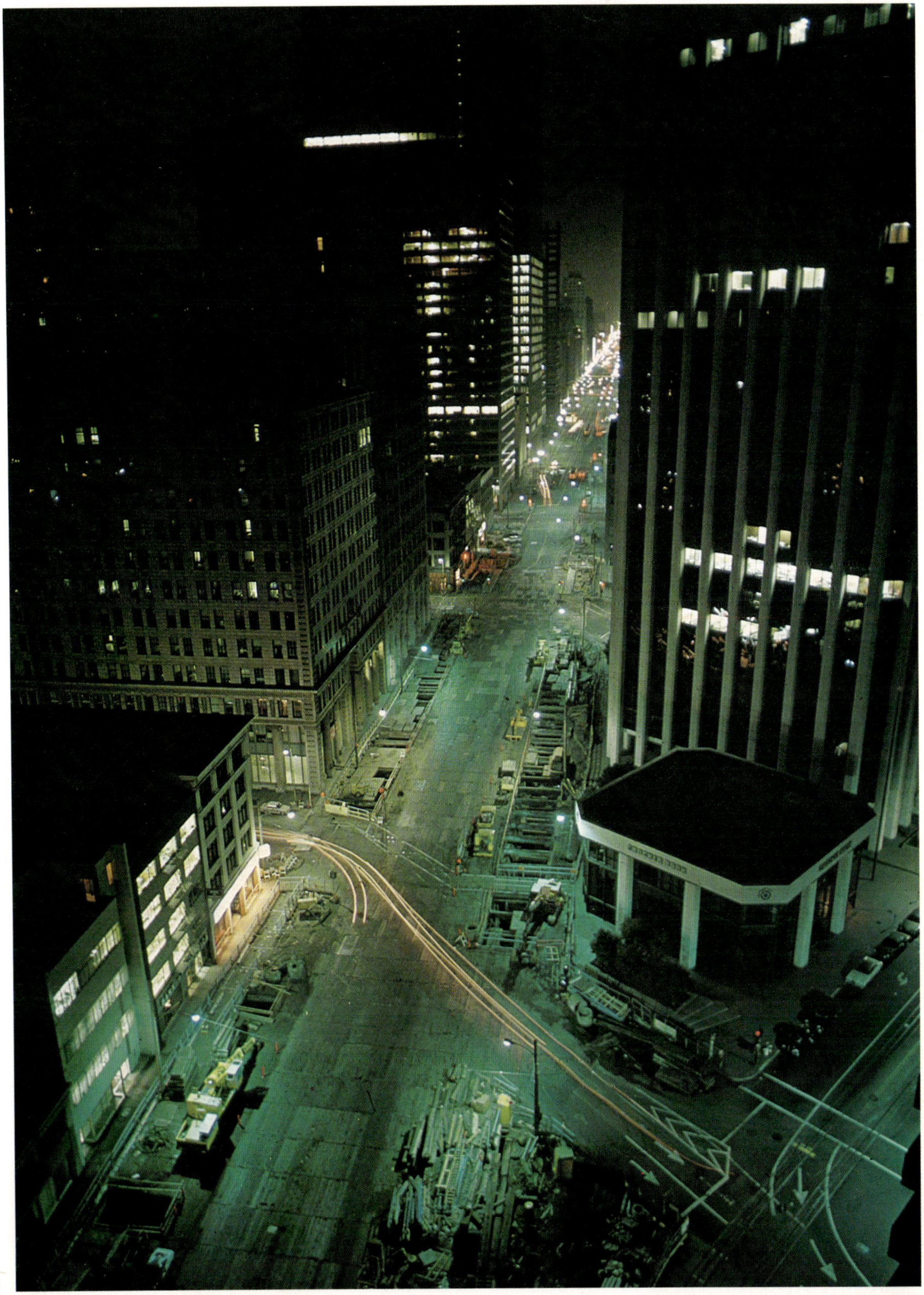

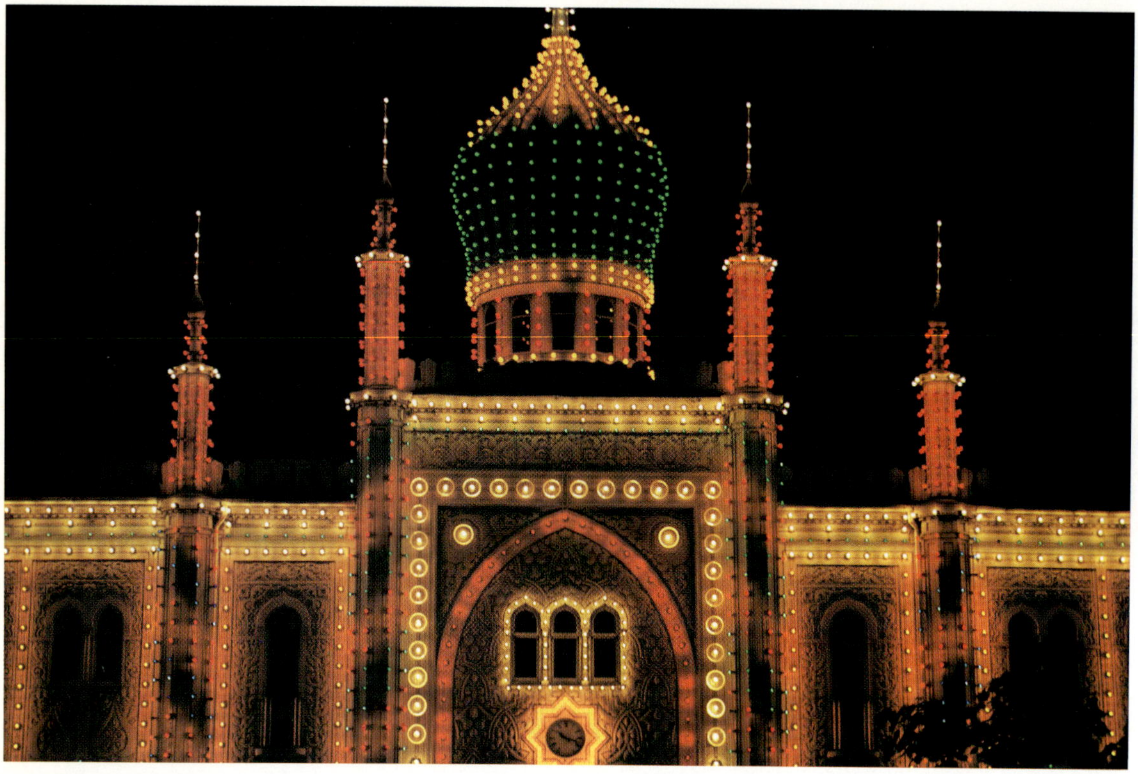

47

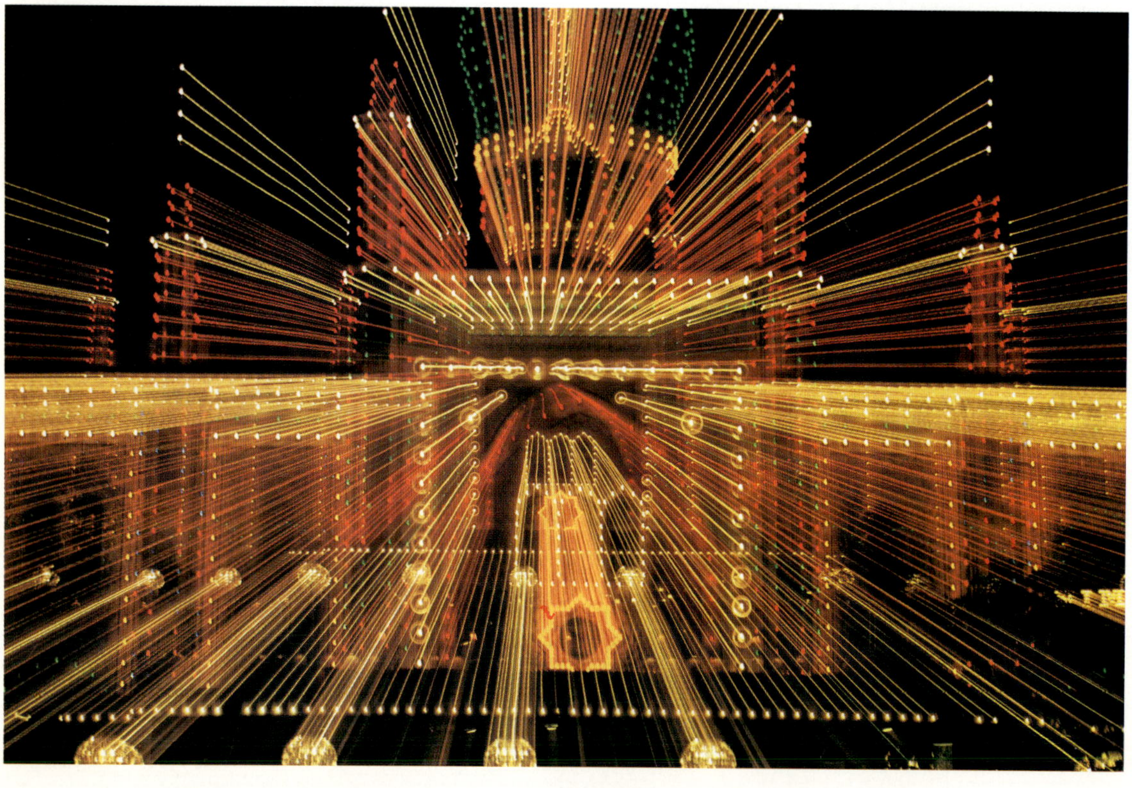

48

49

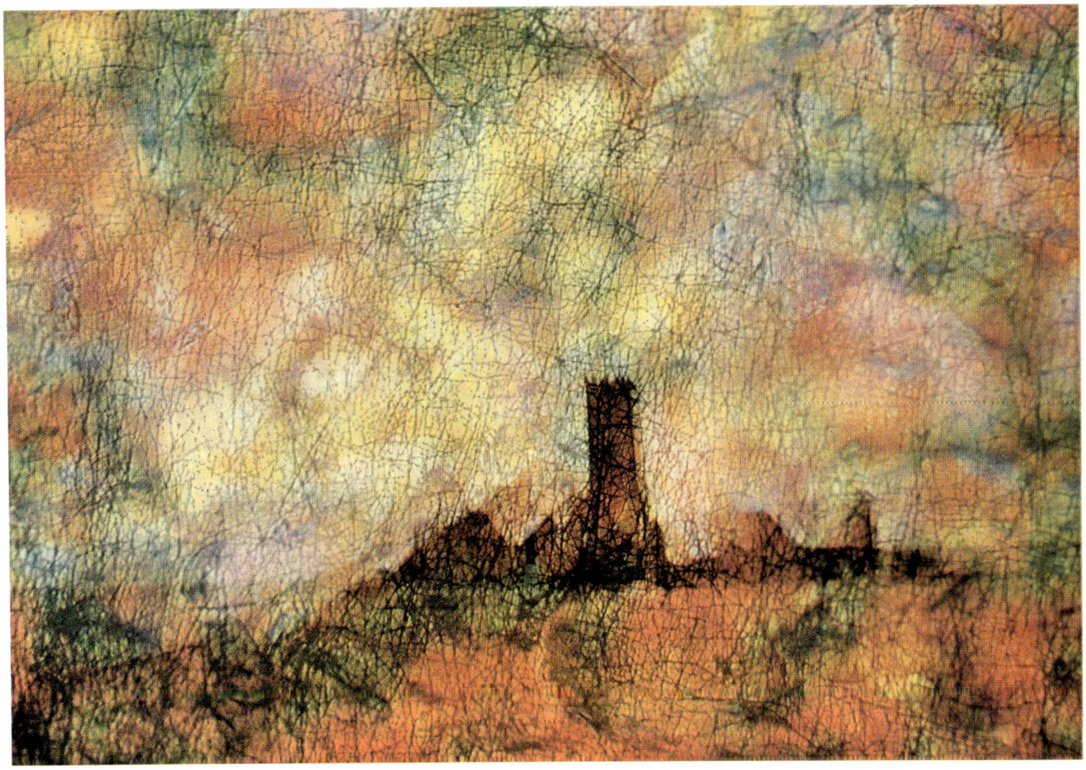

51

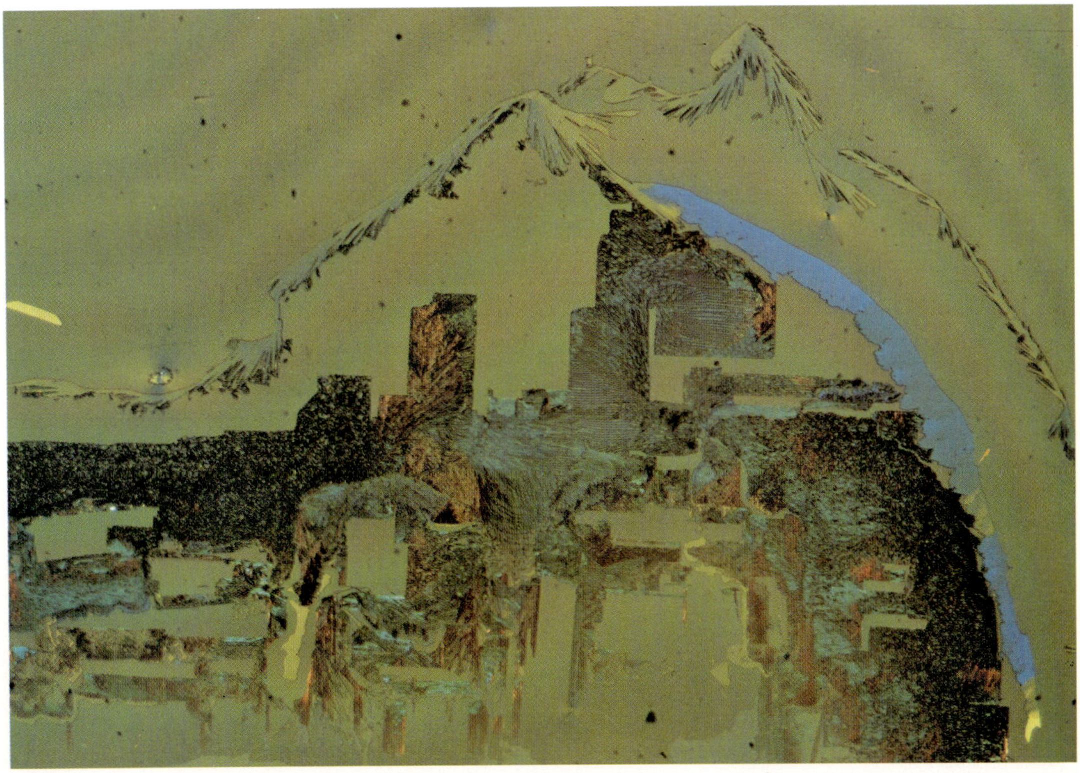

Experimenting with Equal Densities

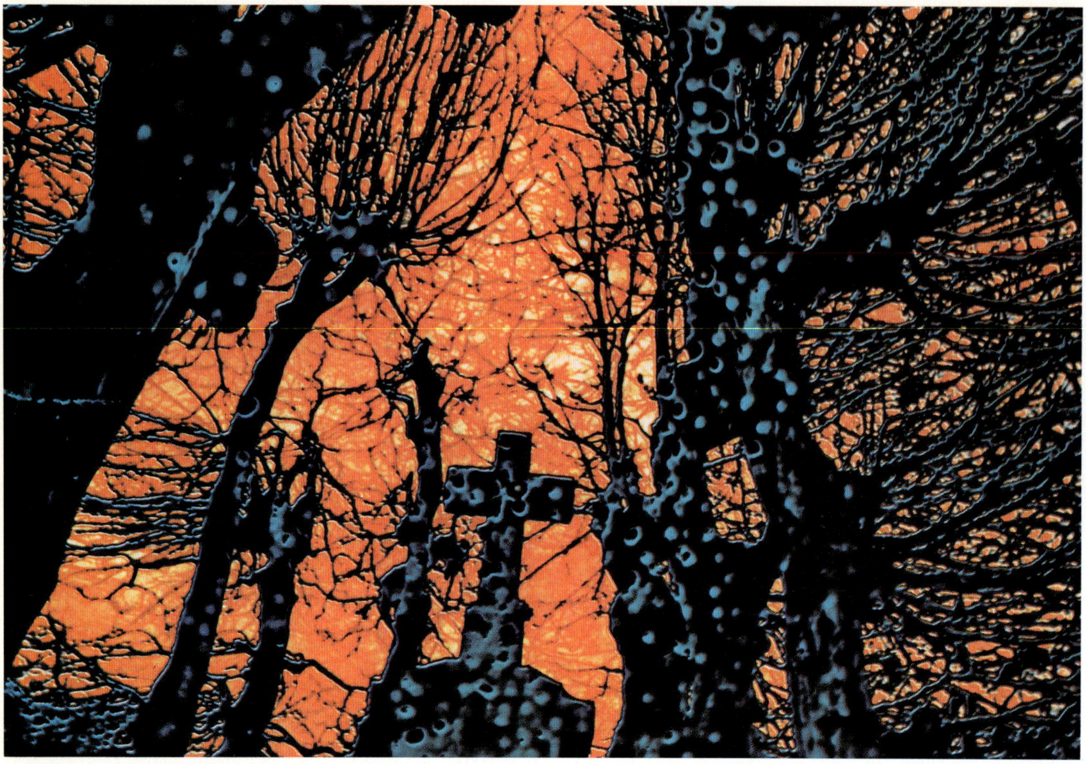

50

Infrared Color Photography

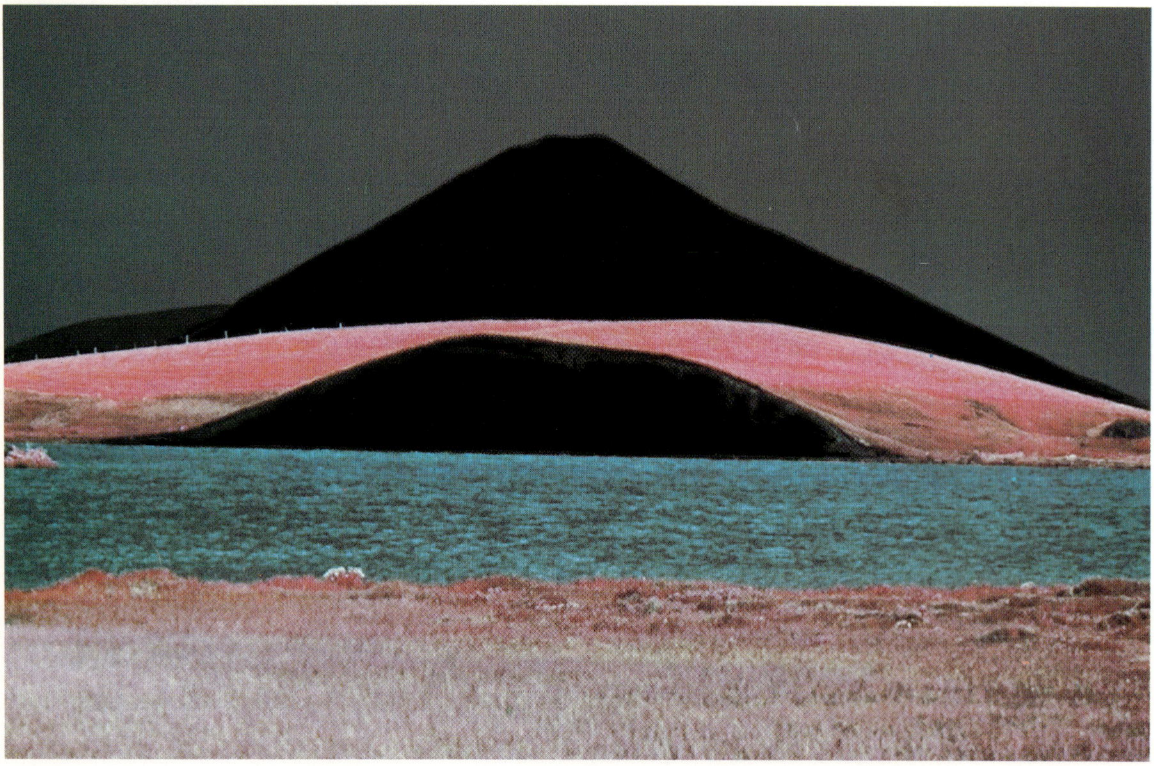

52

Technical Information

The Patterned or Striped Landscape

**Photo 1. "Spring"
Edgar Ollmann, Austria**

Ollmann discovered his subject on a casual walk on the crest road between Hofgastein and Badgastein. The delicate green stripes seemed to be drawn by a painter's hand, and the blossoming cherry trees surrounding the farmhouse seemed an ideal spring setting to him. Yet, a tremendous woodpile next to the house somehow marred the picture, so Ollmann asked the farmer to remove it, which he willingly did. Meanwhile, it had grown late and Ollmann had to postpone his photographing until the following day. Very early the next morning he shot this photo, which he himself considers one of his most beautiful landscapes.

Even the impartial viewer cannot fail to appreciate the aesthetic appeal of this striped landscape, for it is not only the harmonic composition—the contrast between the lively foreground and the graphic background—that attracts the viewer's attention, but above all the delicate shades of neat, green contrasting stripes in the field and the meadow. The pale pink of the roof is hardly a contrast to the green, although green is its complementary color, and the delicate cherry blossoms accentuate the harmony of this spring picture rather than detract from it.

The formal composition is a blend of diagonal and vertical elements: The fields draw diagonal stripes across the picture; the roof and the silhouette of the tree prolong this line, dividing the picture from the upper right-hand corner to the lower left-hand corner; while the trees accentuate the vertical. Only the structure of the meadow at the base of the picture is very detailed and serves as a forceful frame. By choosing a vertical format, Ollmann emphasized the diagonal and vertical elements in his picture. He shot this photo looking down with a 180 mm telephoto lens, which explains why the perspective in depth seems very compressed. Technical data: 1/125 sec. at *f*/8, Agfachrome 50 S film (ASA 50, 18 DIN).

Photo 2. "Meadows"
Heribert Dünzl, Germany

This photo mirrors the stillness of a spring day through clever cropping and composition. The green of the spring meadow is enlivened by the delicate yellow of the dandelions. The marked shadow lines created by the undulations in the ground divide the space into three horizontal areas of equal size. The asymmetrically positioned birch accentuates the top three shadow lines. This photo was composed very carefully. Dünzl confirmed this by referring to the law of the "Golden Mean." "One can observe this law in various ways," he says. "In my picture it is the ratio of 2:3 achieved through the shadow line marked by the tree. The symmetry of the photo is enhanced by the asymmetrical force of the tree, which animates the perfect harmony of horizontal lines, heightening the effect rather than disturbing it. Although the rather formal composition with its straight lines seems somewhat severe, the yellow flowers counteract this and render the friendly warmth of a spring day."

The soft contours in the picture and the minimal shadows indicate that the photographer took this picture on a cloudy day. The aperture setting seems to prove this. Technical data: 1/30 sec. at *f*/11, Agfacolor CT 18 film (ASA 50, 18 DIN). The telescoping reveals that a 200 mm Telyt lens was used. Dünzl notes that he shot this picture from the hill opposite.

Photo 3. "Rapeseed Field in Holstein"
Uvo Pauls, Germany

With the very first sprigs of green in the meadows, the brilliant yellow rapeseed fields lend stark contrast to the landscape. Pauls tells us that 60 percent of the total German rapeseed production is grown in Holstein. This photo would have been a run-of-the-mill shot were it not for the remarkable contrast produced by the prevailing conditions: the sky filled with thunderheads, and the strong sun illuminating the intense yellow of the rapeseed field. The third color in the photo—the rich green in the foreground—adds the key to a vivid composition that evokes a cheerful mood in the viewer. A touch of yellow can enliven a picture, as a comparison with Dünzl's photos (2 and 4) will show. The colors in Pauls' photo are uneasy and dissonant, and the dirty gray-blue of the sky forms an impressive contrast to the yellow rapeseed field. Although green and gray-blue dominate in terms of space, the intensity of the yellow rules the scene. Pauls realized that the breadth of a landscape is intensified by a marked emphasis on the sky, which he captured by using a 35 mm wide-angle lens. By positioning the horizon near the bottom of the picture, he intensified the coloring of the sky. Technical data: 1/250 sec. at *f*/4, Agfachrome 50 S film (ASA 50, 18 DIN).

Photo 4. "Poplars"
Heribert Dünzl, Germany

This cheerful landscape is characterized by the formal arrangement of a row of poplars along a lane. The slightly overgrown wheel tracks in this country lane are very effective graphic elements, for they seem like rails tracing a pattern through the dark green grass. The poplars with their black trunks contrast only slightly with the rich green of the meadow. The branch of a blossoming cherry tree not only serves as an element of form in the right-hand part of the photo but also as an indication that it is spring. Delicate white cherry blossoms brighten an otherwise serene photo and seem to make the green of the grass even greener. The cherry branch takes up a minimal amount of space in relation to the dominating row of poplars. Yet the tonal emphasis of this composition is in the right-hand side of the photo; and the blossoming branch not only enlivens the picture but helps alleviate the mood of the somber, overcast day, making the motif seem more cheerful. The perfectionism in the formal composition and the way Dünzl achieves it indicates experience. The first thing that strikes the viewer is the careful spacing of highlights. Dünzl was very careful to crop the photo so that the gentle curve of the lane terminates in the lower left-hand corner at an angle with the horizontal line of small yellow flowers at the base. He used a 280 mm lens and telescoped the poplars. This compression in perspective resulted in a strong emphasis on the diagonal line of the lane. Technical data: Dünzl used a tripod and exposed for 1/8 sec. at *f*/11 on Kodachrome 25 film (ASA 25, 15 DIN).

Photo 5. "Flood"
Julius Behnke, Germany

There are photo subjects that seem fascinating at first glance but are quickly forgotten. Others take a little time to appreciate and then remain forever in one's memory. Behnke's river landscape is of the latter type. He took this photo in a flooded area in Turkey early in the spring. Spontaneous attention is aroused by the three horses. Only at second glance does one perceive the landscape behind the animals and the delicate way in which the poplars are mirrored in the water. The patterns traced on the surface by the light are an integral part of the atmosphere in this photo.

Everyone who knows the work of this renowned photographer from Wetzlar knows that Behnke is a born landscape photographer and a gifted animal photographer as well—the ideal person for achieving a photographic symbiosis of animal and nature. The harmony of colors is very appealing; the subtle hues of blue, green, and brown set the mood of an early sunless morning. The hint of a pale blue sky is seen as a reflection in the water shimmering through the upper part of the photo, and serving as the upper boundary of this horizontally conceived landscape. The dominating expanse of water is deftly structured through the reflection of the poplars and the line separating the flooded meadow from the rippling surface of the river bed. The three horses dominate the foreground.

Behnke watched them for a while, waiting for the right moment—the proper combination of stillness and motion without awkward groupings. It is no mere coincidence that the three horses stand apart: Patience, concentration, and a deft technique were necessary in order to come up with such a perfect photo.

Photo 6. "South Tyrol" Heribert Dünzl, Germany

Dünzl described this picture as follows: "The last day of a bus excursion to South Tyrol took us to Seiseralm. In was November, and the air smelled of snow. Gray clouds obscured the sun, producing a spectacle of light and shadow. The colors seen through the polarizing filter looked downright dramatic: The sky was gentian blue, the grass in the foreground the color of bronze, and the windswept larches were a golden yellow. The clouds throwing their hasty shadows on the scene added the final touch to this already dramatic scene—a pending thunderstorm, such as is rarely captured even on postcards."

In the chapter on winter photography, the effect of the polarizing filter and its intensification of color are discussed. Essentially, the polarizing filter eliminates the reflections of polarized light present in nature as well as the mirroring effects visible to the naked eye. Since the eye is conditioned to this, it does not consciously register that the slight change in color tones effected through the use of a polarizing filter is actually a slight manipulation of the actual impression registered by the eye. The use of a filter intensifies the color tones considerably and is especially noticeable in the more textured colors in the sky, the gold of the larches, and the gleaming yellow of the burnt autumn meadow in the foreground.

Dünzl favors the classic division of composition into foreground, center, and background, although the dividing lines are full of motion. The varying heights of the larches are counterbalanced by the ridge of the mountains. The dark shadows of the mountainside in the center set up a bright/dark contrast that intensifies the luminescence of the larches. The spacious foreground adds balance to this extraordinarily dynamic composition. Technical data: Dünzl used a 135 mm lens at 1/30 sec. and *f*/8, Kodachrome 25 film (ASA 25, 15 DIN).

Photo 7. "Bulrush" Henning Wulff, Canada

The merits of monochrome compositions—photos with various shades of one and the same color—are discussed throughout this book. In this example, brown tending toward olive-green sets the color tone. The shot demonstrates how little scenery is needed to depict the characteristic traits of a landscape. In this case, the grasses can be found in many places, but here they are symbolic and express the general feeling of desolation in a wasteland.

The decisive element in this photo is the pale blurred light of the sun hiding behind a threatening cloud. It sets the mood and influences the coloring as well as the distribution of emphasis in this photo. One could say that Wulff placed the sun at the only possible spot in his composition: next to the bush at the right-hand side, which dominates the formal structure and virtually encloses the blurred circle of sun with its concave contour. Needless to say, this is what the photographer was after when he chose to position his camera low and focus upward. The 35 mm camera was probably placed only a few centimetres above the ground and was equipped with a 400 mm lens, which explains why the sun seems so large; it appears to sit right next to the bulrush in the foreground.

The asymmetrical composition of this picture is perfect because the focal point—the bush at the right-hand side—was positioned in such a way that all objects and spaces in this photo have a graphic relation to one another. The energy in line and form is balanced out by a toned-down color scheme. A polarizing filter was used for color intensity. Technical data: 1/250 sec. at *f*/6.8, Kodachrome 64 film (ASA 64, 19 DIN).

Photo 8. "The Hoggar Mountains"
Helmut Hermann, Germany

Hermann described the way he captured this photo as follows: "During a trip across the Sahara, I spent some time in Tamanrasset and the impressive Hoggar Mountains. One day before sunset I climbed the highest peak of this range—the 9000-foot-high Assekrems. The sun was setting behind the mountain peaks on the cloudless horizon. The last rays of light, falling almost horizontally, made this spectacular scene glow in delicate hues of gray. I shot a whole series of pictures and, as I discovered later on, this photo renders the mood that I experienced perfectly. The beauty of this picture in my opinion lies in the delicate monochrome shades that become lighter as they approach the horizon."

This photo serves as an excellent example of how haze not only influences perspective and depth but the mood as well. The haze intensifies the quiet calm of dusk. Photos of this type would also be interesting in black-and-white. The mood is set by the warm monochrome colors, starting from a blackish-brown that grows progressively lighter until it merges with the yellowish-beige color of the sky—a sign of the heat of the day that has just abated.

The photo also demonstrates how the size of the mountain ranges determines perspective, for the second range is larger than the first one. Depth is largely simulated by the density and intensity of color, which is a graphic element in this composition. The photographer open to new ideas can take this photo as an example of ways to improve his or her own composition. Technical data: Hermann took this photo with a 180 mm lens at 1/250 sec. and *f*/4 on Agfacolor CT 18 film (ASA 50, 18 DIN).

Photo 9. "Boat in the Fog"
Donald Cox, USA

Cox wrote that he would never forget the gloomy morning on which he took this shot. He had rented a room in a small fishing village on the East Coast of the United States in order to photograph beach scenes. That morning he awoke, chilly, in a strange bed and a strange place. He dressed quickly in order to begin his search for photographic subjects. The weather was miserable—damp and foggy—and he had to protect his camera from the drizzle with his parka. While strolling along the boat harbor in a rather dismal mood, he found a boat anchored in the bay. As he climbed in, he discovered his motif. It recalled all the mysterious ghost stories that his father—a seaman by profession—had told him about this part of the coast. Cox actually felt this uneasy atmosphere on that morning and tried to capture it with his camera.

He mounted a 21 mm wide-angle lens and focused on the dilapidated boats stuck in the mud. The fog seemed to grow denser by the minute, but it was light enough for him to attempt a shot at *f*/5.6 and 1/30 sec. on Kodachrome 25 film (ASA 25, 15 DIN). The picture has remarkable atmosphere and a well-planned graphic appeal. The yellow boat in the foreground divides the left foreground diagonally, and the line of the keel is projected through the rock in the foreground right down to the base of the picture. This vertical line is counterbalanced by the horizontal line seen dimly through the fog in the upper half of the photo. The resulting spatial division in a ratio of 1:4 establishes an arresting relationship between the immense foreground and the small, dimly defined background. The horizontal line is cleverly emphasized by the floating boat in the distance, which reflects the murky surface.

Photo 10. "Tomato Pickers" Thomas Höpker, Germany

Höpker is one of the best-known photojournalists in Germany, famous for his extensive photo-documentation of Israel, which was published in a special issue of *Life* magazine entitled "The Spirit of Israel." This photo is part of the series. Höpker, who studies art history and was an enthusiastic amateur photographer before making a name for himself as a professional photojournalist, is a master at his job. He has been acclaimed as one of the photographers best able to portray emotional scenes. This simply means that even working with symbols—which he loves to do—he composes a picture with dramatic force and conviction. This particular photo serves as a good illustration of his style.

Höpker shows the characteristic topography of a tomato field in Israel. By focusing on the tomato pickers in this field, he blurred almost two-thirds of the picture: The area in sharp focus extends from the horizontal line of the pickers upward toward the horizon. Höpker photographed directly into the sun, which caused bright reflections on the plastic covers protecting the tomato plants. The circular patterns of these reflections indicate that Höpker used a reflex lens, which is increasingly popular among photographers lately. The horizontal line that looks like a silver ribbon is not a river, as one might suspect at first glance, but the accumulation of countless plastic tents. The light/dark contrast dominates this photo, creating a strong and forceful impression: Meadows, a lane through the fields, and a row of trees are barely discernible in the background, and the dark violet of the sky frames the picture at the top.

Photo 11. "Fallen Tree"
Heribert Dünzl, Germany

A violent autumn storm felled this tree and sent it crashing into the pond—a symbol of dying nature. The pale shimmer of the reed grass visible only as faint copper patches in the foreground also speaks of things transient. The reeds beyond the frozen lake are in focus, though Dünzl chose the willow rather than the reeds as the focal point in the picture. The colors here are subordinate to the graphic design traced by the tree. The black of the tree trunk melts into the blue-gray of the shimmering ice and the pale brown of the reeds—a sign of late autumn.

Despite the tree's dominance, the classical division into three planes is clearly recognizable. Space and tonality are almost equally balanced: The bright foreground is followed by a slightly darker center (the reed grass) and the vaguely discernible forest in the background, each varying only slightly in brightness of color. Yet they create a terrace-like effect—a progression from bright to dark.

Obviously the main elements contributing to the atmosphere of this picture are the time of day and the handling of light—catching the reflections on the ice and the glowing copper patches of the reeds in the foreground. All these elements create a rather mellow mood in this pale-hued autumn scene. The concentration in depth was achieved with a 200 mm lens; the clear delineation of sharp and blurred zones is attributed to opening the lens all the way. Technical data: In spite of the hazy lighting conditions prevailing that day, this shot was taken at 1/250 sec. and *f*/4 on Kodachrome 25 film (ASA 25, 15 DIN).

Sunsets

Photo 12. "Golden River"
Kees van den Berg, Holland

Van den Berg's attitude toward a sunset determines the viewer's reaction when looking at the photo. And it is unimportant whether the sun itself is part of the picture or visible only as a reflection on water, ice, or snow. In this nocturnal river landscape, as in most sunset scenes, the expressiveness of the colors contrasts with the graphic lines of the sharply defined details in the landscape. At first glance, such a shot seems simple to take—both as far as composition and the handling of light are concerned. And in fact the purely technical side poses relatively few problems provided one has the necessary practical experience.

The difficulty lies in the creative approach—in selecting just the right moment when optimal light conditions prevail and in acting quickly at that very moment. A good eye and inexhaustible patience are essential prerequisites in this endeavor, because not every evening produces such spectacular golden colors, and only rarely does one see such a pale red glow—an important color component in this photo. A careful look reveals seemingly unimportant details which, in fact, were deliberately incorporated into the picture (for example, the faint reflection of a passing steamer and the seagull in the foreground).

Van den Berg focused on the brightest part of the water shimmering under the evening sun for a light reading and then followed the prevailing tendency to slightly underexpose in order to achieve the rich golden tones. He was careful to preserve enough detail in the reddish hues in the background and to retain the tonal spectrum in the silhouette of the village, which offers a gentle contrast to the black islands dividing the river. The shot was taken from quite a distance with a 400 mm telephoto lens, which compressed space to such a degree that everything is sharply delineated from foreground to background. Strong contrasts and reflections on the water look as if the photo has been "softened," thus heightening the mood and atmosphere of this twilight scene. Technical data: Van den Berg used a tripod with a shutter speed of 1/125 sec. at *f*/6.8 on Kodachrome 25 film (ASA 25, 15 DIN).

Photo 13. "Evening Sun on the Arctic Ocean" Susanne Baden, Denmark

Such a photo seems a gift even to the professional photographer. But this photo did not take itself—there was work behind it. Baden, the wife of a Danish photographer, took part in an expedition to the western coast of Greenland organized by the Worldlife Foundation. This journey was of special significance to her because it marked the start of her career as a photographer. With camera in hand, she aided her husband in his search for the white-tailed eagle. They combed the reefs, rocks, and icebergs along the fjords of Greenland in a boat and had ample opportunity to take beautiful color pictures. The varied and often spectacular light conditions were a never-ending temptation to take yet another photo, especially of sunsets in every possible variation.

The picture reproduced here is one of her most beautiful memories, says Baden. She took it looking down with a 400 mm lens because, in her opinion, this lens is best suited for unusual scenery—both in rendering light as well as coping with composition. As in André Martin's photos (21 and 22), the compression of details in the distance contributes significantly to the dynamism of the formal composition.

The in-depth expansion of the photograph is visible not only in the perspective reduction of details but also in the shadowy contours of the icebergs delineated in ever finer contours in the distant haze. The contrast between the silhouettes and the expanse of water and sky glowing in the deep gold of the evening sun creates the graphic quality of this photo. The focal point is the iceberg in the foreground, which stretches across the entire picture, thus subordinating all other details and elements while accentuating the horizontal. The distant mountain range visible through the haze is its counterbalance in terms of form. The classical division into three planes—foreground, center, and background—is applied and brought out here. Technical data: Baden selected her frame with utmost care and worked with a tripod, exposing for 1/125 sec. at *f*/6.8 on Kodachrome 64 film (ASA 64, 19 DIN).

Photo 14. "Deluge"
Marc Champollion, France

The golden gleam of the setting sun is captured here in this shot of water pelting down on huge boulders. The picture is intriguing because one wouldn't expect the sun to shine in the midst of a torrential rain. The effect is so convincing that weather conditions appear to have been extraordinary that day. But slowly it will begin to dawn on the viewer that there is something fishy about this picture. This is by no means a sun-drenched deluge but rather the result of a simple trick; it is actually water spraying from a fountain on a square in Copenhagen, which Champollion, a teacher, took at very close range. He adds, somewhat tongue-in-cheek, that his pictures rarely show things as they really are.

Champollion loves to paint with light and considers this fountain picture a successful example of how to go about it, adding that the combination of light and water is one of his favorite subjects. One has to admit that his artful dodge worked perfectly. It serves as an excellent example of how one can use the sun as a medium; that is, show it indirectly and thus capture the mood of a sunset by using it as a sort of converter. Water is best suited for this purpose, as demonstrated by Photos 12, 13, 16, and 20.

The bright colors in Champollion's deluge indicate that the sun was still far from entering the deep purple phase that is characteristic of dusk. The sunlight falls into the picture horizontally from the side, rather like a spotlight, putting the backs of the rocks in deep shadow. These rocks look like huge boulders because Champollion photographed them at very close range with a telephoto lens. Technical data: In order to emphasize the effect of falling water, Champollion used a long exposure time (1/15 sec.), which permitted him to set his 90 mm lens at *f*/16 and get additional depth of field on Agfacolor CT 18 film (ASA 50, 18 DIN).

Photo 15. "Silhouette"
Kees van den Berg, Holland

The danger of getting too much of a good thing is greatest when photographing sunsets. Therefore, it is important to "mold" the gleaming masses of light in order to bring out the juxtaposition of light and shadow. Van den Berg shows us how this can be done in his photo with the revealing title of "Silhouette."

Silhouette implies the complete reduction of contents into

form, though form should not be the only element. By waiting virtually until the very second when the sun touched the earth before releasing his shutter, van den Berg created an appealing picture characterized more by the dense quality of the sky than by the sun itself. Drenched in dark brownish-purple, the sky forms a perfect backdrop for the foreground—which resembles a stage setting—and the trees—which appear to have been cut from black paper. The spiritual relationship between this type of photography and the enigmatic landscapes of the nineteenth-century German painter Caspar David Friedrich immediately comes to mind.

This is a very poetic photo, and van den Berg is known to be a master of such moody pictures. He demonstrates that it pays to "shape" atmosphere. Translating the contents of this picture into words would require a reference to the unusual light as well as to the aesthetic appeal of the composition and the perfect rendition of even the smallest detail.

To begin with, there is a dense black area in the foreground that is emphasized by the fine outlines of the trees taken asymmetrically into the picture. Even though the focal point is at the right-hand side of the picture, it is the bright sun—which is relatively small in size—that arrests the viewer's eye, and it is here that the color scheme in the photo starts. The intense red border surrounding the white disc of the sun animates the picture. The glare is so intense that the silhouette dissolves here. One should remember this when dealing with similar motifs and situations. The horizontal cloud formations reflecting the last rays of the sun serve to counterbalance the upward motion of the silhouetted trees. Technical data: Van den Berg took this landscape with a 135 mm lens and set the shutter at 1/250 sec. with an aperture of *f*/11, using Kodachrome 25 film (ASA 25, 15 DIN). Experience and an extremely sensitive eye for special lighting conditions led him to choose this extremely short exposure time. The silhouette-like effect was achieved by deliberately underexposing.

Photo 16. "Sunset"
Thomas Höpker, Germany

In this photo, man as the measure of all things is an integral part of the landscape (also see Photo 10). This silhouetted human figure hurrying along the beach is the continuation of a diagonal line originating at the upper right-hand corner of the photo. The fact that the figure is walking out of the picture is no cause for criticism here but rather shows good judgment on the part of the photographer. The casual appearance was neither planned nor arranged by

Höpker; instead he captured this figure in the right place of his composition at the right moment.

Formalists should note that the cut-off edge on the left-hand side has its justification here, proving once again that a compositional flaw can be transformed into an essential element of the design. The narrow strip of sky above the horizon indicates that Höpker did not tilt his camera, as one might assume. A second diagonal—the line between the sand and the water—is accentuated by the figure, and an imaginary zigzag pattern of diagonals can be traced right to the horizon at the top of the picture.

The composition is asymmetrical, the focal point being the rock in the sea (right-hand side) illuminated by a dark yellow stream of sunlight traveling vertically through the picture. In contrast to the sunset shown in Photo 13, Höpker's picture is dominated by the shadowy zones. But since these are not of an intense black, the whole scene is bathed in a yellow glow, as if the photographer had used a contrast-reducing yellow filter. This strange light sets the mood of this picture, which is not a gay one but rather speaks of the threat of darkness—the fear of approaching night.

Photo 17. "Sun Games"
Bert Kühn, Germany

A photographer trying to avoid conventional sunsets sometimes uses very strange devices. Kühn himself admitted that he used a rather unorthodox approach: He shot the sun while lying down in the grass through a bush of anemones. He was trying to "deform" the perfect round of the sun in order to get an original photo instead of a slick one. The resulting woodcut-like flowers dominate a large section of the photo, the sky behind them glows in muted orange, and the small blotch of sun deformed into an egg-like shape glares through the grass like an intruding spotlight. Silhouettes of various size and density are outlined against the dark orange-red edge of the sun. The orange of the sky has merged into a strange purple in the section between foreground and background where the flowers are. It is interesting to note how the varying degrees of sharpness seem to add depth and dimension to this picture (in reality only a few centimetres), for Kühn opened his 180 mm lens to *f*/2.8. The blurred zones around some of the plants are due to the gentle breeze blowing during the hand-held exposure—1/30 sec.

What does this picture demonstrate? An original portrayal of an everyday motif requires an original approach and careful computation of apertures and exposure times. Though it may seem simpler to follow tried-and-true methods, they are outmoded for the advanced landscape photographer who is trying to realize his or her own personal ideas.

Photo 18. "Cap de la Chèvre"
H. Jürgen Neumann, Germany

This impressive picture won first prize in a major international photo competition. Rightly so, one must admit, for it merits comparison with many prize-winning masterpieces of color photography. This sunset on the Atlantic Coast of France once again proves the contention that the secret of good composition is simplicity of form and a harmonious, gentle color scheme. The mood and poetry of this picture are due to the simplicity of approach. The contrast of the red sun traced with delicate strips of cloud animates this serene picture and enlivens the fine tones of this ice-blue color scheme. Neumann admits that his "dream photo" is not only the result of expertise but also of long-awaited luck in finding such an ideal subject.

When the decisive moment arrived, he had to act fast, for within seconds the sun would disappear completely. This is how Neumann describes his photo: "Ever since I started taking photos, atmospheric conditions have fascinated me. Maybe this is due to the fact that I studied geography. I have photographed many sunsets during the last few years, working with various apertures and lenses, from a 15 mm Hologon to a 400 mm Telyt, and using all sorts of filters. Last summer I was in Brittany, and one afternoon at dusk I walked to the Cap de la Chèvre. The slightly hazy blue sky and the small lighthouse reminded me of the periscope of a submarine and seemed to promise a very special photo. So I hurriedly put my 280 mm lens on my camera, anchored my tripod securely on a rock, and set the aperture slightly below the reading on the light meter. I wanted the sun to be rather dark in my photo, so I tried 1/8 sec. at *f*/4 on Kodachrome 64 film (ASA 64, 19 DIN). I did not use a filter, because I wanted to catch the mood as it really was."

Neumann chose a symmetrical division of space. He divided and accentuated the horizontal, letting the slightly darker sky that divided the picture in two parts hang into the lower part. This placed the tonal as well as the spatial emphasis in the upper part of the picture, which is accentuated by the asymmetrical placement of the sun in the upper section. The protruding lighthouse in the lower left-hand part of the photo serves as a counterbalance to the sun.

Photo 19. "Sunset in Iceland"
Helfried Weyer, Germany

There are widely traveled and seasoned photographers who claim that the most beautiful sunsets occur in Iceland. Photography itself, of course, can neither prove nor disprove this thesis as the sunset photos reproduced here demonstrate. Which of these sunsets do you consider the best? One thing is clear: The short, half-hour-long nights in Iceland in midsummer offer a spectacle of the most extraordinary play of colors. A bizarre landscape and dramatic cloud formations, as well as a clear atmosphere are bound to produce brilliant photos. It is no wonder then that visitors to Iceland bring home numerous sunrises and sunsets—photos that fascinate by their sheer beauty, intensity, or gentleness.

Weyer, who became known as a world traveler through his lectures on Leicavision, submitted an excellent example of the typical clouds over Iceland. The sun shines like a white disc on the landscape silhouetted against the light, and bizarre blackish-orange clouds float in the sky. The bright edges of the clouds bring out their shapes even more sharply. The cloud in the upper right-hand corner of the photo has special weight in the overall composition and, together with the disc of the sun, counterbalances the row of houses in the foreground in the lower left. It is interesting to note how the sun seems to eat its way into the foreground with its glowing red halo.

Unfortunately, Weyer did not provide precise technical data, but it looks as though he underexposed slightly in order to bring out the intensity of the evening sky as a contrast to the black silhouette of the landscape. He used a Leicaflex SL camera with Agfacolor CNS film (ASA 80, 20 DIN).

Photo 20. "Monsoon Sky"
Dr. P. V. Katrecha, India

Katrecha, the doctor who submitted this photo, is a member of the Leica Club of India. Sea motifs are among his favorites, he says. The monsoon sky shows that he saw this landscape rather the way a graphic artist would. This formalistic and very personal composition is heightened by the colors of the evening sky. There are two reasons why pictures such as this one have to be taken with a tripod: First, at this time of day (dusk), one has to allow for a longer exposure time (in this case 1/30 sec.); and second, selecting a frame that renders all the details exactly as is desired cannot be accomplished without a tripod—in fact one should not even try it. In addition, placing the camera on a tripod enables the photographer to select the aperture best suited to rendering perfect perspective and depth of field. This is especially important when dealing with finely delineated details, such as the sailboats in the foreground and center. Even the most delicate clouds in this monsoon sky are in focus.

Metering light in cases where the sunlight is merely reflected in the sky, flooding the scene with light, poses very few problems. There is about as much light in the sky as on the water, so one can more or less rely on the readings of the exposure meter. Since light diminishes rapidly at dusk, the photographer must act fast once the sun has vanished beneath the horizon. The tendency in photos like this one is to slightly underexpose in order to get the silhouette-like quality of the boats. If it is already rather late one can do the opposite and overexpose slightly in order to get color luminosity such as in this photo and avoid too much black in the picture. Technical data: Katrecha used a 135 mm lens and exposed for 1/30 sec. at *f*/5.6 using Kodachrome 25 film (ASA 25, 15 DIN).

Emotional Photography

Photos 21 and 22. "Impressions"
André Martin, France

The landscapes taken by the French photographer André Martin are strongly influenced by French impressionist painting and were first exhibited by Kodak during Photokina 1974. His photographs—two of which are reproduced here—demonstrate a very personal technical approach as well as a distinct painterly view. The feeling of intimacy conveyed by these landscape miniatures is due to unusual lighting situations, such as overcast sky, haze, fog, and bad weather. Martin often takes photos at dusk when the sun is just disappearing behind the horizon. Such lighting conditions call for long exposure times; most of these scenes are taken from a tripod with an unusually long-focal-length lens (400–1000 mm), or with a reflex lens of extreme focal length. Paradoxically, Martin likes to use these lenses for close-ups, which is why his photos show such compression in the perspective of detail as well as intensification of color. The reduction of light caused by these lenses is sometimes considered a handicap by photographers, but Martin takes advantage of this by deliberately using long exposures–1/30, 1/15, or 1/8 sec.

The fact that he uses wide-open lenses is obvious in the two pictures; in both, only small sections of the motif are in sharp focus. The dominating elements in his photos are seldom in the foreground and are usually juxtaposed to a larger blurred zone. The theme of his picture—the motif—is usually wedged between a large blurred foreground and a background similarly out of focus (Photo 21). In Photo 22, the background is sharp, while the foreground and center are blurred. This also helps to create a feeling of depth. Sometimes Martin achieves additional blurring by moving the camera slightly while exposing; in other words he favors streaking effects, a popular device among sports photographers. Martin also likes the effects created by a breeze in grass and branches and deliberately employs all these techniques, at the same time controlling the extent and intensity of blurred zones in his composition.

Photo 23. "Spring on the Seaside"
Heribert Dünzl, Germany

This Mediterranean scene (the island of Brac on the Adriatic Sea) is a fine example of how similar photography is to painting. The technique looks like an impressionistic pointillist painting, while the strong, rich colors recall the landscapes of the German painter Emil Nolde. Nolde translated nature into abstract forms and concentrated on bringing out the atmospheric feeling, just as Dünzl has done in his photo. The turquoise of the sea provides a lively contrast to the yellow of the Scotch broom, which takes up two thirds of the photo and carries its message: spring on the seaside.

Dünzl took great pains to get the coastline, beach, and surf into focus while deliberately blurring the yellow foliage. The contrast of the two complementary colors—yellow and blue—is matched by the contrast between sharpness and blur. The intensity in color is due to the use of a polarizing filter. This filter and the position of the sun (at a right angle to the line of focus) dimmed the reflections from water and landscape causing a blackening at the edges of the turquoise sea, eliminating texture almost completely there. This in turn helped to bring out the white of the foam along the beach and the sand-colored curve of land. The narrow, almost black horizontal strip of sea along the upper edge of the picture is counterbalanced by the diagonal of the coastline.

No doubt you will be surprised to learn that this coastal scene was taken with a 90 mm lens, to which the picture owes its dynamic perspective. It influenced composition as well as the degree of blurring in the blossoms. Also note the care Dünzl took in placing the two yellow dots into the blue of the sea. Technical data: Since the polarizing filter "swallows up" considerable light, he had to expose for 1/60 sec. at *f*/5.6 in spite of the bright sunshine. He worked with a tripod and used Kodachrome 25 film (ASA 25, 15 DIN).

Photo 24. "Cherry Blossoms"
Herman Stöcker, Jr., Germany

This landscape still life has a certain degree of poetry about it, even though the subject is a typical spring motif—cherry blossoms. The color composition in Stöcker's picture is very special. It looks like a Japanese watercolor, and owes its charm less to the objects pictured than to the vibrating dots of color that convey the spirit of a spring day.

This photo appeals to the viewer's imagination since the branch in the foreground is blurred to such an extent that it is impossible to make out the details—the blossoms could easily be flowers. Numerous petals dot the surface of the pond under the branch. Some have already sunk and are visible only as diffused purple and brown spots marked by subtle blue reflections of light. The picture also speaks of the short-lived joy of spring.

The juxtaposition of two planes characterized by bright/dark contrast and sharp/blurred zones demonstrates a talent for original composition. Hardly visible, yet effective as a color stimulant, is the fresh green of young leaves shining through the pink of the blossoms and the blue of the water, all of which seem to have been touched by the hand of a painter.

Photo 25. "Winter Sun"
Wim Noordhoek, Holland

Noordhoek is known as a man who sets up his camera when all the others have started packing up their gear. For years he has favored dusk, the late evening light, and hazy or foggy landscapes. Available light is his secret. The Dutch "photo professor" takes his pupils for walks along the dunes of the North Sea on cold, soggy weekends, or roams the islands off the coast of Holland in search of subtle motifs. And during a slide show, it is with great enthusiasm that he describes how some of his transparencies were shot under "impossible" lighting conditions.

The winter sun depicted here was taken in 1965 and belongs to his early phase. In those days, anyone handling or ignoring depth of field and sharpness as Noordhoek did was considered either an avant-garde photographer or simply somewhat crazy. But what exactly is so avant-garde in a photo such as this one—his treatment of form and color, his penchant for monochrome color shades, his seeing and focusing on things that other photographers would not even notice? Noordhoek's unusual way of looking at a scene—the intimacy of a basically unattractive view of the pale winter sun through a tangle of branches—involuntarily draws the viewer into this photo. It is a view we have all beheld when roaming through the woods and the fields. And why did Noordhoek think it worthy of a photo? That is for you, the viewer, to decide. This personal experience is revealed as such in the photo; it is the conclusion reached when viewing Noordhoek's work. Absolute mastery of the camera and its accessories is a basic prerequisite for transforming ideas into pictures that can speak to the viewer.

Noordhoek divided his photo into three planes: the diffuse tangle of branches in the foreground; the delicate tracery of leafless winter trees and bushes behind it; and the distant sun, which serves as a point of focus and color contrast at the same time. Technical data: The exposure time of 1/15 sec. at *f*/5.6 on Agfacolor CT 18 film (ASA 50, 18 DIN) is an indication of how little light Noordhoek had at his disposal when he pressed the shutter to take this superb photo.

Photo 26. "Rainy Day"
Rudolf Auer, Germany

This photo was described by a renowned photo expert as "a masterpiece of the still young medium called color photography. It is subtle, sophisticated, and demonstrates mastery in handling color." One can only agree with the opinion of the photo aesthete and should merely point out that this judgment was made back in 1971. Though color photography has advanced greatly in term of technical aids, Auer's "Rainy Day" has lost none of its relevance and can still be considered exemplary in the field of modern color photography. There has been a lot of talk about Impressionism in the past years, and some seem to think that this term excuses anything blurred and out of focus. This, of course, is not the case.

Auer's photo captures the impression of a rainy day in such an artistically calculated blurred fashion that quite a few amateurs might wonder whether this is actually a photo or a painting. But it is precisely the "natural" rendition that creates the effect of an impressionist image, just as a good water color would. This proves that a painterly element—in whatever form—does not necessarily mean manipulation in photography. Who would blame Auer for using photography in order to express emotions? And why exactly should a photographer experience nature differently from a painter?

Auer took this photo from above through a rain-streaked window and exposed for 1/60 sec. at *f*/4 on Ektachrome X film (ASA 64, 19 DIN). He moved the camera slightly in order to achieve the blurred, streaky effect in the picture. The more distant the details, the more effective this technique is, as the row of houses in the background shows. Auer not only moved the camera sideways but also up and down, as the orange signpost in the left part of the photo reveals. The diagonal lines in the street ending in a narrow strip of wall at the left edge of the picture are the determining graphic elements in this photo. The clever selection and arrangement of these elements created a window-like effect, for the wall of the house ends in a bluish-black blurred zone (probably a windowsill). The view looking down onto the wet, almost empty street offers an ideal vantage point from which to capture the delicate color reflections of the houses and the lonely stroller whose red umbrella serves as an animating element. The purity of the colors is amazing, and even the gray sky is mirrored in the asphalt.

Photo 27. "On the Námaskard" Hans Schiffmann, Germany

Iceland is a paradise for amateur photographers, especially landscape buffs. Sulfur fumes gushing up from hot crevices swirl above the high plateau of Námaskard in northern Iceland, an area that is visited by countless Icelandic travelers including those who fly to the Arctic Circle simply to photograph. Hot springs formerly used for sulfur production gush up from deep within the earth. Today this is one of the many sights in an untouched part of the world where one can also study the geological history of the earth. The rough lava-encrusted earth is unusually colorful. Sulfur yellow, purple, and even poison-green-colored patterns mark the earth and make this area a utopia for color photographers. Heaven and earth are in motion; dramatic cloud formations and steaming geysers animate the torn surface of the earth, creating an almost sinister atmosphere that might well be haunted by gnomes and spirits.

Schiffmann tried to catch the bubbling of a hot spring and its crystalline deposits in a close-up, and he also wanted to capture the broad expanse of a landscape enveloped in steam. He succeeded through his clever choice of framing—the spring in the foreground against the relatively sharply defined landscape in the background. The big mudhole in the foreground with its contrasting light and dark tones in which the pale glow of the sun is mirrored is the focal point. The tonal contrasts in the center and background are softened by the steam floating low above the ground. The light of the hazy sun is caught in places in the steam and the clouds.

The color wheel in this motif is a mixture of blue, green, and the ochre of the earth, resulting in a strange, oppressive monochrome that even the blue of the sky and its blue-gray rain clouds does not cheer up.

Composition is of interest, too. The high format is cut by several diagonal lines starting in the foreground and terminating in the horizon, expressing a certain rhythm—a kind of pattern of tiers moving upward to the mountain ridge where they culminate. This divides the picture horizontally in a ratio of 4:1. Foreground, center, and background are clearly defined. Technical data: Schiffmann took this photo with a 90 mm lens, at 1/125 sec. and *f*/8 on Kodachrome II film (ASA 25, 15 DIN).

Photo 28. "Sun Above the Gulfoss Falls"
Helfried Weyer, Germany

Iceland's most spectacular waterfall, the Gulfoss, is only 90 minutes from Reykjavik by car. It is mentioned in every travel brochure and poster on Iceland. But when it is depicted, it is usually shown in its entirety—the overwhelming masses of water cascading downward. For an overall view, one has to use a wide-angle lens. Weyer did not attempt to photograph the entire waterfall, however. When he noticed the fantastic rainbow, he decided to make it the subject of his moody photo. He wanted to capture the rainbow without losing the effect of the masses of water rushing down. So he acted quickly, focusing on the gurgling whirlpool dotted with reflections from the sun.

The rainbow rising from this small zone is sharply in focus and travels upward amidst a cloud of spraying water. By using a telephoto lens, Weyer concentrated on the very few but decisive details in his motif: the mossy green rock in the foreground; the cloud of water spraying up behind, which gradually diffuses into a wall of fog; and the sharply defined cliff in the upper right-hand corner.

The refreshing quality of this picture is due to the clever juxtaposition of the monochrome bluish-green of the scene and the spectral colors of the rainbow, as well as the contrast between sharp and blurred zones. Note how the rainbow seems to be reflected in soft hues in the bluish-green zone in the upper left-hand corner of the photo.

Photo 29. "Anglers"
M. Zimmermann, Holland

This photo was telescoped much like the Noordhoek picture (Photo 25). Two fishermen in a boat with their backs to the photographer are seen through the maze of blurred branches in the foreground. This binocular effect creates the impression of intimacy, since the anglers are completely unaware of the photographer watching from the background. The same feeling—that of secretly observing a scene—is transmitted by this photo.

The composition is almost identical to Noordhoek's photo, too. The difference, however, lies in atmosphere. While Noordhoek's winterly sun looks cool and almost melancholy, Zimmermann has succeeded in catching the loveliness of a sunny spring day in his photo. The sun appears as a soft golden shimmer where the boat is anchored, and is reflected in the glow of the red canvas chairs. The intense green of the blurred leaves tempers the yellowish cast of the water where the sun is shining, resulting in a pleasing color contrast between the boat and the cold, bluish-green of the branches. A wide-open 200 mm lens allowed the photographer to capture marked sharp and blurred zones — the sharp zone takes up only about a quarter of the total area right around the boat.

The viewer may profit from photos like this one by realizing that: (1) the courage to approach motifs in an unconventional manner produces unique photos, (2) the overriding monochrome tones in a picture can result in intensely colorful photos, and last but not least, (3) a daring but resolute mixture of blurring and depth of field are basic elements in successful color photography.

Photo 30. "Forest Lake"
Heribert Dünzl, Germany

This picture is for romantics—a picture that conjures up spirits and elves. And learning that it was taken in the moorland of the Bavarian Forest near the Czechoslovakian border brings to mind the mysterious sagas and stories for which this isolated and lonely region is known. Dünzl, who has already shown his cool aesthetic nature (Photos 2 and 4), reveals the romantic side of his character here—a dream-like picture meant for dreamers. But whether cool or romantic, one can always detect his tendency toward the careful realization of his photographic concepts. His own description offers further insight on the photo: "The forest is mirrored in dark mysterious pools. The clouds drifting overhead make one think of a moonlit scene, but it is actually the sun that is reflected on the water. As is often the case, a polarizing filter was an important aid in rendering the magic of this scene; it enabled me to carefully select the atmospheric elements I wanted to include in the picture. The tripod enabled me to divide my photo precisely and allowed for longer exposure times. A wide-angle lens (in this case, a 28 mm Elmarit-R, *f*/2.8) sometimes results in slightly distorted pictures while a tripod lessens that danger."

Unfortunately Dünzl forgot to mention exact aperture and exposure. The relatively great depth of field suggests a small lens opening. He focused on the reflection in the water, for the gentle contours of the firs are visible in sharply delineated detail. The fluffy clouds in the sky are also well defined in the reflection. On the other hand, the mossy foreground and the plants in the water are also perfectly sharp, indicating that the depth of field extended from the immediate foreground to the most distant objects (the fir trees). Generally speaking, when shooting a reflection (in water), one must focus on the reflected image itself and not on the surface of the water. The distance from the camera to the reflection and the distance from the reflection to the object being reflected must be added together when computing apertures. An extensive depth-of-field zone was necessary in order to bridge distances and get the entire picture in sharp focus. This was achieved with a 28 mm wide-angle lens which, when set at *f*/8, renders everything between 5 feet (1.5 metres) and infinity in focus.

Snow and Ice—Form and Color

Photo 31. "Snow-Covered Forest" Heribert Dünzl, Germany

Since the inception of photography, forests have been a favored theme, so it is not easy to find new and interesting variations on the motif. Attempting to take an entirely original and completely new approach would mean never shooting at all. Naturally, the photographer recognizes certain similarities with famous photos when looking through the viewfinder, yet every picture can be taken only once, and each particular landscape setting is original.

Winter subjects in particular have a transient quality about them, and often seem on the verge of melting in the sun or dissolving with the rain from one minute to the next. In Dünzl's photo, the snow covering the forest like a layer of white powder softens the contrast between the dark green of the fir and pine trees, the light brown of the forest floor, and the rust brown of the beech trees. The rounded contours of the beech trees stand in contrast to the pointed conical shape of the evergreens.

In such photos the sharpness of detail is very important. Of course, the amateur shooting a forest scene thinks first of the picture as a whole, yet it is the structural details with their individual forms and colors that give the picture its distinctive character. A successful forest landscape must be completely in focus. Dünzl achieved this with a 200 mm Telyt lens on his Leica. Technical data: He used a tripod, an exposure of 1/8 sec. at *f*/11, and Kodachrome 25 film (ASA 25, 15 DIN).

Photo 32. "Ice Towers in Peru" Dölf Reist, Switzerland

Reist is one of the most successful mountain climbers in the world, and is famous for climbing Mt. Everest. He asserts that the purely technical photographic skills involved in taking his impressive pictures were less of an obstacle than the mountain climbing required to find such settings. The major difficulty is synchronizing physical and emotional energy to take a good, well-composed picture after the exertion of the climb.

Reist is not interested in documentary shots free of emotion, but strives to take pictures that are lovely and also indicative of the joy the mountain climber experiences in this once-in-a-lifetime view from the top of a conquered peak. Of course, similar photos can be taken from a helicopter or an aerial cable car with much less physical exertion. But this is why Reist is so proud of his photos. The widely discussed problems of "blue snow" ceased to be an issue for Reist a long time ago.

In the regions over 16,000 feet (5,000 metres)—the ice towers of Quitaraju in the Cordillera Blanca, Peru, are 18,700 feet (6,000 metres)—in the purest air imaginable, the blue of the sky, snow, and ice is of an incredible intensity. To filter this away while shooting or later in printing would simply be "falsification." Reist generally shoots without a filter, unless it is necessary to protect the camera from blowing snow or ice. Then and only then will he mount an ultraviolet filter—which absorbs ultraviolet light—on the lens. Reist knows only too well that any additional glass in front of the lens diminishes the sharpness. Only on rare occasions, when glaciers or reflecting ice interfere with his aims, will he use a polarizing filter.

Arriving at the correct aperture is a major problem for a mountain-climbing photographer, due to the extreme amount of available light. Reist uses two methods for combating this difficulty: When he is not overly exhausted, he spot-meters various details of the mountain landscape with the help of a selective light meter and averages the different readings. His years of experience in mountain photography then stand him in good stead. When he is too tired to do this, he works with a normal light meter using a 27-degree angle of incidence, and varies the setting slightly for a second and third shot. His photo of Quitaraju was taken in this way with a Leica and a 90 mm lens. Technical data: 1/250 sec. at *f*/11, Kodachrome 25 film (ASA 25, 15 DIN).

Photo 33. "Shadowplay Against the Light" Hugo Schöttle, Germany

When snow covers the countryside, when meadows, fields and paths lie buried beneath a blanket of white, the time has come for a graphic picture with the simple forms of bushes, trees, and their shadows. The few shapes emerging from the snow can be arranged quite easily; the entire landscape is seen at a glance. Furthermore, the question of color composition becomes much less of an issue. The snow has a delicate hint of blue in the sunlit areas, while the shadows of the bushes and trees have a definite azure tint.

Schöttle took this shot in full sunlight, when the interfering ultraviolet rays cause a strong "bluing" effect. It should be pointed out that he did not judge exposure according to the color temperature of the light but rather by the length of the shadows, particularly of the birch trees. The midday sun was a necessary prerequisite since he wanted to capture the open area between the evergreens in the foreground and the two birch trees in the center.

The interplay of forms is also emphasized through the classic division into three distinct planes. In the lower-left foreground, it is the massive spruce that forms the basis of the composition together with its shadow. The arrangement is asymmetric and the eye moves from the lower left, to the upper right, to the group of trees in the background, which are slightly to the right of center. The contrast in both form and texture between the shaggy spruce in the foreground and the silhouetted group in the background creates a feeling of open space. Since Schöttle took this shot with a 180 mm lens on a Leicaflex SL, one can imagine the amount of telescoping achieved here. Technical data: 1/250 sec. at *f*/11, Agfachrome 50 S film (ASA 50, 18 DIN).

Photo 34. "Cross on the Summit" Hans Huber, Germany

Snow-covered pine trees are a subject well worth shooting, since snow often lends the trees a completely different shape. The view of a grove of snow-clad young trees, or a lone proud fir, can be a rewarding photo, yet the photographer searching for an original subject may have a difficult time finding what he or she wants. Perhaps the best approach is to stand back and review the scene—look for original juxtapositions or arrangements. The form of the cross rising from the peculiarly formed snowbank was the inspiration for this photo. With a secure sense of what makes a good picture, Huber positioned the cross in front of the calm, peaceful dark blue background of the sky. He achieved a very personal picture by using a long-focal-length lens, (200 mm), and by placing the branch of the fir tree in a sunny section, directly in front of a broad shadowy area. The total effect is one of exceptional contrast.

The snowbank is delicately and precisely defined in the background but somewhat fuzzy in the foreground, indicating that the source of light is not a blazing sun. Huber confirms that the sky was slightly overcast, which also explains the minimal blue cast on the snow. In order to avoid a perfectly symmetrical arrangement, the cross was positioned somewhat to the right of center at a slight incline. Asymmetry is stressed by the strong diagonal of the supporting snowbank. As a balance, Huber placed the green fir branch in the lower right-hand corner, slightly out of focus. It provides a color contrast to the blue-green of the shadowy forest in the background. Technical data: 1/ 500 sec. at *f*/2.8, Kodachrome 64 film (ASA 64, 19 DIN).

Photo 35. "Hoarfrost"
Hugo Schöttle, Germany

Once again, the blue of the snow is clearly visible. Were it filtered away, the photograph would no longer reflect what the eyes really see. This photo of a parched hemlock twig covered with hoarfrost was taken early in the morning when the first rays of the sun fell on the shadowy blue carpet of snow. The excellent lighting conditions contributed decisively to the picture's superb quality. Only intense sunlight hitting the twig from the side could make the frosty crystals so luminous, explaining why Schöttle chose the earliest possible time of day for his shot. By positioning the frost-covered twig against the dark blue shadow zone, the luminescence is intensified. In such light, frost crystals on the ground also appear particularly three-dimensional.

There is another reason for the early morning hour: Only at this time do the frost crystals "growing" in a leftward direction receive the direct light of the sun, just the situation that created the stunning luminous effects. This explains why images of this kind cannot be photographed at any time of day, as the dictum "the main thing is the sun" might lead one to believe. The proper amount must be carefully selected, too. Without a doubt, the early morning light is the best possible prerequisite for frost since the crystals are quickly melted by the rising sun. On very cold days, the late afternoon and evening sun may be just as favorable, depending on the line of focus.

The precise positioning of the frosty twig in the viewfinder was simple here. The subject was placed somewhat to the right, with the intention of avoiding the boredom of a symmetrical arrangement. In conclusion, it is important to choose a subject that is simple in form but full of contrasts. Technical data: Macro-Elmarit-R 60 mm *f*/2 lens with a Leicaflex SL, with a shutter speed of 1/250 sec. at *f*/4 on Agfachrome 50 S film (ASA 50, 18 DIN).

Photo 36. "Couple"
Heribert Dünzl, Germany

This delicate, nearly monochrome golden-brown composition is a superb example of what a little imagination can do with two frosty snail shells. Naturally, the pleasant effect is due in large part to the golden light shining on the glistening hoarfrost crystals. A little maneuvering was required to capture this photo, since in reality the two snail shells were not so conveniently and harmoniously positioned. After carefully and tastefully arranging the shells, Dünzl became somewhat carried away with his imagination and decided to manipulate the natural colors as well. The tranquil harmonious background—the brown tones of the earthen floor—with a myriad of sparkling ice crystals were taken into careful account.

At first glance, it would seem that the golden tone of the snail shells is a reflection from the brown earthen floor, but in reality, there was some outside assistance. Since the illumination of the sun was missing, a piece of gold foil was used as a reflector in order to illuminate the snail shells, thereby also bringing out the hoarfrost crystals more clearly. Color is well balanced between the gold of the shells and the earthen tones of the forest floor, and the shadows provide the desired three-dimensional effect. Technical data: Tele-Elmar 200 mm *f*/4 lens, with a universal adapter and a Visoflex 3, on a Leica camera using Kodachrome 25 film (ASA 25, 15 DIN).

Photo 37. "Ice Abstraction"
Heribert Dünzl, Germany

After years of experimenting, Dünzl discovered that a polarizing filter not only reduces reflection from a glossy surface but also increases the transparency of ice or water, provided the camera is held at the correct angle. An angle of 30 to 40 degrees should exist between the reflective surface and the line of focus. The result is this photo called "Flying Saucers."

If you did not know it was an ice-covered surface, it would be very difficult to make out what this picture really depicts. Probably the bizarre shapes attracted Dünzl's eye in the first place.

A lively imagination and a keen eye, as well as a curiosity about peculiar and distinctive abstract motifs, are essential for successful landscape photographs. But shooting such subjects requires a good bit of experience, technical know-how, and a good sense of design and composition.

The inexperienced observer would be inclined to compare these abstract forms to some familiar object. These frozen air bubbles might appear to be peculiarly formed chessmen or a squadron of flying saucers. The trained eye, however, takes pleasure in the engaging interplay of forms. Perhaps the eye will even see the white frost-fettered bubbles on the surface as tiny white clouds suspended above a dark abyss. Technical data: 135 mm lens on a Leica camera. Other details are unknown.

Photo 38. "Rime Frost"
Heribert Dünzl, Germany

This maple seed pod, which looks like an insect from a distant fairy-tale world, was spotted on a frozen side channel of the Danube. There was no time to lose, for the rising sun was quickly approaching this patch of ice. Soon the sun's warmth would destroy the magic. So, the camera was quickly placed on the tripod. . . and to work! Dünzl, an experienced photographer, knew that a polarizing filter would be helpful here, so he mounted it to his 135 mm lens, with a universal adapter for close-ups, on his Leicaflex SL. With this combination, he was able to approach his subject to 100 centimetres and enlarge it. (The photo seen here is a life-size rendition.) The polarizing filter eliminated the reflection from the ice and altered the texture of the surface, transforming it into a smooth, homogenous, nearly black background.

The delicate frost crystals and frozen air bubbles stand out clearly against the contrasting color. These air bubbles are constituting elements of the composition and the ice crystals enliven the otherwise calm surface. In addition, the polarizing filter intensifies the color of the seed pod and helps to bring out its delicate design, making it appear slightly molded. The white shadows beneath the pod look like insect legs and create the feeling that it is actually floating above the surface of the ice. Three of the five frozen air bubbles are mirrored, which gives the picture a tremendous three-dimensional effect, despite the fact that the actual zone in sharp focus is only a few millimetres.

Dünzl does not recall precise technical data, but he used a gray card, which facilitates accurate light metering in critical situations, and he chose the smallest possible focal length for optimal sharpness.

Photo 39. "Rainbow in Ice"
Heribert Dünzl, Germany

The photo reproduced here is Dünzl's favorite from a collection of similar motifs. Only Kandinsky could have created such a color composition, he claims, since Kandinsky was instrumental both as a painter and as a theoretician in freeing painting from pure representation.

Except for the use of a polarizing filter to intensify the rainbow's colors, Dünzl's photograph of air bubbles trapped in a frozen pool of water is a true rendering of the scene as it appeared in nature. He describes the creation of this photo as follows:

"Persistence and luck were the decisive factors: persistence in pursuing an imaginative idea and luck in being in the right place at the right time. For several winters, I have looked at melting ice through a polarizing filter searching for interfering colors. It was with this intention that I came to this frozen pool near a construction site. The unusual form and arrangement of the bubbles in the ice attracted my attention. The polarizing filter revealed an unexpected array of colors. Apparently the water in this pool was mixed with oil, at least that is the only explanation I can find for the tiny liquid islands trapped in the ice. These islands, melting more rapidly than their surroundings, created the lovely rainbow effect. Precise data are not available, but I stopped down the lens considerably for greater depth of field and I used a Telyt 200 mm *f*/4 lens with an adapter on the Leicaflex SL."

Dünzl's description of this photo seems relatively simple, and it may be that an amateur wishing to capture a similar scene can master the purely technical aspect rather quickly. But the creative approach involved in selecting such a detail from a frozen pond cannot be passed on quite so easily. The colorful rainbow effect is the result of interfering colors that are often found when oil and water mix. The reduction of polarized light brought about through the use of the polarizing filter caused an intensification of color. Moreover, careful adjustment of the filter enabled the photographer to select the rainbow pattern that he found most aesthetically pleasing, and even the reflection from the surface of the ice and the frozen air bubbles were taken into account.

Photo 40. "Forest Path"
Hermann Roth, Germany

The quieter the colors he chooses, the more intimate seems Roth's relationship to color on the whole. To find color where it is reduced to very few but distinct, clearly defined tones requires special sensitivity toward both form and color. In pictures such as this one, the sensibility of the photographer and his or her personal feeling for nature are clearly visible.

Roth, a well-known Munich photographer, writes that the contrast between the rigid forms of the trees, the gentle fluttering of the reeds, and the unmarred white surface of the forest path inspired him to take this shot. His comment concerning the suppressed vitality of this forest scene seems somewhat contradictory, yet the characteristic quality of a photo cannot really be described more accurately.

There is a certain suppressed energy in the strong graphic quality—in the relationship between the path, the reeds, and the trees. The golden rust color of the grasses and the dark, blue-green iridescence of the trees lend a liveliness to the picture as does the contrast between these colors and the white snow-covered path. The contrast is enhanced by the dynamic perspective and the course of the path, broken by two patches of brown earth, as it tapers off into the distant background. The grasses lining the path become gradually smaller in size, creating a very marked three-dimensional effect. In short, the picture owes its liveliness to the two contrasting colors—namely blue and orange—and to the strong contradictions in form due to composition and perspective.

The relatively long-focal-length telephoto lens (200 mm) further contributed to the perspective. When a shot is taken from a distance, this lens produces a strong depth concentration and telescoping effect. The varying degrees of sharpness between the foreground and center are also achieved with the telephoto lens. The otherwise tranquil character of the photo is encouraged by the absence of strong contrasts in light. Technical data: 1/30 sec. at *f*/4, Kodachrome II film (ASA 25, 15 DIN).

"Cityscapes" and Experimentation— Aesthetics in Precision

Photo 41. "New York"
Julius Motal, USA

The photographer who aims at capturing the characteristics of a city has an easy time of it in New York. Examples are in abundance, for this city has been extensively photographed. A wide-angle lens is almost a must there. Only on rare occasions has a camera been so successfully directed skywards to capture one of the typical moods of this city. The picture has a threatening quality about it, because the facades taper so steeply and seem to crush the onlooker beneath their weight. The eerie gleam of the steel giants and the dark sky rent open by the blazing sun also contribute to the menacing mood. The reflection caused by the blinding glare of the sun was deliberately taken into the composition. In the upper right-hand corner, where you least expect it, is a branch of an acacia tree creating the illusion that the top is perhaps the bottom and vice versa. If you view the picture from the side, you will see that this illusion is not so out of the ordinary.

The intensity of the monochrome, blue-violet composition is due to the polarizing filter and the use of an extreme wide-angle lens (21 mm). By eliminating the greatest proportion of the polarized skylight, even the blue of the sky seems to have turned black, approaching the tones of the facades. The trail of an airplane, which cuts diagonally across the picture creating a powerful contrast to the towering steel structure, is probably accidental, although the white trail fits well into the photo. Technical data: 1/60 sec., *f*/16, Kodachrome 25 film (ASA 25, 15 DIN).

Photo 42. "Facades"
Josef Kaufmann, Germany

The amateur cityscape photographer will probably not want to attack the most difficult architectural problems immediately. Interesting facades offer the beginner a good opportunity to become familiarized with the subject. The photographer who first masters this area will have an easier time with difficult subjects later on.

Kaufmann found this row of different facades in Sydney and cleverly transformed it into an attractive pattern. The contrast between today and yesterday—between traditional and modern architectural styles—lends this picture its special character. The strong telescoping of the vertical lines and the concise and precise treatment of the subject indicate that a telephoto lens was used. Since vertical lines are the dominating factor in this picture, there was no question that the format should be a long rectangle. By squinting and viewing the picture, you will see the facades melt into one another in a series of vertical stripes.

This photo makes another point as well: It is more interesting to let both old and new facades exist one next to the other than to tear down the older structures. There is a beauty in mixing old and new, in integrating the old in a new architectural concept. The contrast is aesthetically pleasing.

Kaufmann waited a long time for the proper light—for this even, nearly shadowless illumination. He waited with good reason, since strong sunlight would have cast shadows, destroyed the delicate hues, and transformed the lively facades into a confusion of indefinable lines. Technical data: 135 mm lens from a great distance at a position above the level of the street, 1/125 sec. at *f*/8-*f*/11, Agfachrome 50 S film (ASA 50, 18 DIN).

Photo 43. "Intersection"
Siegfried Hartig, Germany

The atmosphere in a photo reflects the human experience of a scene. However, many people may wonder whether this applies to cityscapes. Yet a somber, completely detached and impartial view of a facade cannot begin to convey the cold, the fog, and the frosty chill in the air as effectively as this view of a traffic light shrouded in haze. Hartig's aim was to capture the typical atmosphere of an early November day rather than the traffic light itself. This mood is quite familiar to the landscape photographer who deals primarily with nature shots. It is less common in cityscapes, however, despite the fact that people are much more strongly influenced by nature's moods than by the rather unexciting architectural structures that have become boringly familiar. There is a reason why the surrealists generally chose a somewhat bizarre metropolitan atmosphere as the setting for their paintings.

Or perhaps Hartig was looking for a means of reflecting his

own personal, somewhat despondent frame of mind. Perhaps he even had the intention of subjugating this mood through a photo. In any case, he has taken a well-balanced shot both in terms of form and color.

The black outlines of the traffic light and the other traffic signs form the focal point in the midst of the hazy silhouettes of the church and the other buildings. The streetlight on the left offers a weak counterbalance to the weight of the traffic light. Though not positioned in the foreground, it is still relatively sharp with good detail. The camera was focused on the only bright color among the range of gray-blues and blacks: the amber of the traffic light. In a formal sense, the traffic light is the most important object—the focal point—and all other lines and surfaces stand in relation to it. It is worthwhile noting these relationships—the overlapping and intersecting surfaces and lines. Technical data: 1/125 sec. at *f*/5.6, Agfacolor 18 film (ASA 50, 18 DIN).

Photo 44. "Steel Works"
N. G. Beheler, USA

The advantages of haze, smoke, fog, or even rain for certain night shots have been mentioned, and Beheler's photo serves as an excellent example of this. Even though pictures like this one might enrage the environmentalists, the amateur photographer can still take pride in a photo that captures the night atmosphere of an industrial plant with such accuracy. Lustrous red clouds of smoke climb across the night sky, illuminated by exhaust fumes, spotlights, and the lights of the steel works. The contours of the buildings form a jagged, angular pattern in the foreground. A feeling of tension is created by the relationship of the various details to one another.

The formation of the clouds and smoke constitute two thirds of the photo, while the firm, angular contours of the plant make up the remaining part. The diagonal division of the photo from upper left to lower right is counterbalanced by the massive smokestack of the blast furnace in the middle of the picture. Oddly enough, the only deviation from the otherwise monochrome red tone of the sky occurs precisely here at the green cluster of glowing lamps. Although it is not an important detail in itself, it becomes the focal point of the night scene. Beheler took this shot with a 135 mm lens from quite a distance. Technical data: 1/125 sec. at *f*/8, Kodachrome II film (ASA 25, 15 DIN). The exposure time was brief and the aperture fairly small indicating that Beheler tended toward underexposure, to ensure that the steel works appear as dark silhouettes.

Photo 45. "Lightning"
Pierre Sauser, France

Many photographers intrigued by a summer thundershower have risen in the middle of a sultry summer night to try and capture the bizarre form of the lightning—the ghostly gleam over the rooftops. But this is a tricky task—a matter of now or never—and if something good comes out, it is usually by coincidence. This is unfortunate, since it really pays to consider techniques beforehand. Perhaps this example and brief description may provide the stimulus for theoretically preparing you to capture a thundershower one day. Perhaps even the knowledge that such attractive pictures may be the result will serve as incentive enough.

A thundershower usually gives a warning of its arrival, so the necessary preparations can be made well in advance: selecting the appropriate lens, choosing a motif, and so on. As in this photo, the subject must of course include a large expanse of sky. You may use a normal ASA 50 or 64 (18 or 19 DIN) color film; either tungsten or daylight film will do, although a sensitive high-speed film offers the possibility of stopping down your lens even further. With subjects such as this one and a wide-angle lens (the photographer used a 35 mm for this shot), you can stop down completely without sacrificing sharpness. Choosing correct exposure time is no problem either. You can use a long exposure time as when shooting pictures of firework displays and take advantage of the old trick of protecting the open shutter against undesired light by covering it with a hat until the appropriate moment arrives. When a spectacular flash of lightning occurs, you simply remove the hat. The trick, of course, is to choose the exact moment and to remember to close the shutter after the procedure.

Photo 46. "San Francisco"
Hans H. Haug, USA

This shot of Market Street in San Francisco captures the magic of a city at night. It was taken from a window of a skyscraper with a 21 mm super-wide-angle lens. The exaggerated slanting lines are caused by the lens, but they do not detract from the picture since they tend to make the buildings seem to lean away from the street. This in turn makes it appear as if you are viewing the picture from the top through a pair of binoculars. This dynamic perspective is emphasized by the street that tapers dramatically away into the background. This is truly an exemplary work of composition.

Complete control of form is a prerequisite for a valid statement of content. There is little traffic meandering through the brightly lit streets, and only a few lines of taillights cross at the intersection. The night seems calm; lights appear in only a few windows, indicating the lateness of the hour. The huge construction site is well outlined as are the numerous parked cars. Thanks to the wide-angle lens, nearly the entire picture is in sharp focus, far into the background where the series of lights begins to converge. The illuminated street provides sufficient light so that even details of the facades of the buildings can be made out. Technical data: 6 sec. at *f*/3.5, a tripod, and tungsten film (ASA 160, 23 DIN).

Photos 47 and 48. "Zoom Effect"
Günter Osterloh, Germany

The streaks and blurred effects attainable with a zoom lens are well known. Unfortunately, the technique has been used rather arbitrarily and only occasionally does one see a picture where its use is justified. Success requires a precise idea of what is to be captured as well as technical mastery of zoom lenses. As an incentive, these two photos offer an excellent example of what can be done. This shot of an oriental-looking hotel facade was taken at night from a tripod. The zoom effect created an unrecognizable abstraction of brightly colored lines. The intriguing quality of this picture is due in part to the bewildering form and also to the intensity of the colored lights. Reality has taken on a purely decorative aspect. The lover of abstractions will undoubtedly find this picture enchanting. It is decorative and would be very effective hanging on a wall.

Such precision can only be achieved when working with a tripod. Nevertheless, Osterloh exposed for a full second with an open lens, zooming across the entire spectrum from 80 to 200 mm. It takes special skill not to move the camera during zooming. Whenever possible, the subject should be positioned in front of a dark background so that the zoom effect is not marred by other sources of light. The light meter reading is usually accurate, provided the background and the subject are more or less equally well lit. When the background is darker, a larger lens opening should be chosen; when it is lighter, one should underexpose slightly (one to two stops).

Photo 49. "Sandwich"
Serge Chirol, France

Sandwich photos are the result of combining experimental shots and mounting techniques, whereby two slides, or a slide and a black-

and-white negative, are superimposed. It may sound simple, but producing an interesting shot is not as easy as it sounds. Chirol has this to say about the technique: "I use every technique available and try to keep everything as simple as possible. The best technique is the one that is not detectable. The most important thing is not how the picture was produced but rather the impression it leaves with the viewer." Of course, this last statement applies to all photos, not just to those produced by sandwiching.

For this intensely colorful picture, two slides were mounted one on top of the other, with the two emulsion sides together, in order to achieve maximum sharpness. The one slide depicts the landscape with a castle; the other, the structure of colored paper, which serves to intensify the colors and break up the structure of the first slide. The combination produces an attractive, nearly abstract color composition that is scarcely recognizable as a photograph. The bright color palette reminds us of Delauney or Kandinsky. The photographer is also convinced of the artistic quality of his photos.

Whether photography of this kind can be called art is something each person must decide for himself. One thing is clear: Pictures like this one are no mere coincidence. The end product must be kept clearly in mind when planning and shooting slides. Often a lot of experimentation is necessary before the desired effect is achieved. Sketching the desired picture may be a good way for a beginner to approach the task of isolating the different pictorial elements.

The subject chosen is usually also the focal point. In Chirol's picture, it is the landscape with the tower. Exposure deserves special attention here, for you must keep in mind that both pictures should complement each other. The intensity of color and form desired determines whether to underexpose or to use a longer exposure time. Just as the formal details—lines, structures, and surfaces—must complement each other, so must the density of the montage pictures be chosen in their relation to each other. One consolation is that this technique sounds more complicated than it really is.

Photo 51. "Vision of a Micro-Landscape" Jörg Piper, Germany

Fantastic scenes are waiting to be discovered beneath the lens of a microscope. They often bear a striking resemblance to landscapes in the "visible" world. An enthusiastic young biologist from Bonn, Jörg Piper, experimented with his microscope until he was able to set up a system by which he could capture any attractive pattern he wanted on film. If you have ever tried to photograph biological specimens under a microscope, you know that it can be problematic.

Piper describes the development of his "landscape" as follows: "The material used was sodium sulfate, which crystallizes quite easily. I placed a drop of solution on the slide of my microscope and let it dry out under the cover glass, where it spread into a thin layer, the density of which corresponded exactly to the depth of field of my lens. I modified the growth of crystals through the use of additional solution until I attained the pattern I wanted. By experimenting, I discovered that even the drying time influences the pattern of the crystal structure. The degree of precision of the microscope plays a decisive role in the quality of the pictures as does the appropriate light. The microscope should not only be equipped with a drying lens and an oil immersion lens, but with exchangeable light- and dark-field condensers as well. The use of a polarizing lens increases the scope.

Piper took his shots with a Leicaflex SL camera, using a Leitz Dialux-microscope and Agfachrome 50 L Professional film (ASA 50, 18 DIN). Is this a landscape photograph? Why not? The world of the invisible is a landscape in its own right and one that has been largely unexplored by photographers.

Experimenting with Equal Densities

Photo 50. "Equal Densities"
Hugo Schöttle, Germany

Many say that color photography begins in the darkroom. This is definitely true when the technique in question is *density slicing*, for this is essentially a printing technique involving color reversal. The darkroom, and to a certain extent the light box, are the places of action. Details of this technique are described in Chapter 7.

This picture was created by adding colors to a black-and-white negative. Three density slices were selected for coloration, and special attention was given to choosing colors that correspond in brightness to the contrasts in a normal positive. The dark tree trunks became black, the reflections caused by drops of water clinging to the windshield of the car were made blue, and the grayness of the gloomy day was transformed into a friendly orange. The process of density slicing with Agfacontour Professional film produces these slices from the original. Each slice is given a different color and the three are then mounted in a sandwich.

The final product was photographed with color slide film. The result is the transformation of a shot of a depressing rainy day into an attractive composition of color and form. Naturally, a different color combination could have been chosen. The special Agfacontour film that makes this special technique possible requires special processing. The subject can be a negative, a slide, or a print, but it should be taken with the idea of density slicing in mind.

Infrared Color Photography

Photo 52. "Infrared Crater Landscape"
Julius Behnke, Germany

This shot was taken in Iceland, at the famous Mývatn, "Mosquito Lake," one of the favored spots for biologists and geologists from around the world. The innumerable species of birds attract the biologists, while the geologists are drawn by the wide variety of craters that can be found here.

Behnke is a well-known animal and landscape photographer. Although generally not much for experimenting, he does like to use Ektachrome infrared film occasionally for special shots. And no wonder, when he can produce pictures like this one. If you know Iceland, you will immediately appreciate the accuracy of Behnke's transposition of color into the infrared spectrum in this picture of Iceland's volcanic landscape (that is, as far as atmosphere is concerned).

The peculiar colors are very striking, and despite the dissonant hues and the lack of all rules of color composition, there is a certain sense of harmony. The liveliest color is the pink of the grass patches, or perhaps this is a pale magenta—a combination of red and blue between the two massive silhouettes of the black volcanic peaks. This pink borders directly on the water, which is blue tending towards cyan. These two bright colors are positioned in the center between the softer colors of the foreground and the dark, blue-green of the sky. The dark forms of the peaks seem to tone down the screaming contrast, yet in effect they emphasize the areas in the center where the two colors border directly on one another. Technical data: Behnke used an additional yellow filter on his 90 mm lens, and exposed for 1/125 sec. at *f*/5.6 with Ektachrome infrared film (shot at ASA 64, 19 DIN). Working with this film is really not difficult. To use it well, however, requires an active imagination and the technical knowledge of the peculiarities of infrared film in terms of color and chemicals. The structure and functioning of this film is explained in detail in Chapter 8.

Index